Liked

Liked

Finding the acceptance that matters most

Ben Thompson

to m,
for going crazy with me

to e and j,
above all, be

Table of Contents

1

The Journey Begins

My Journey Began with Shame and Despair

By the time I was six years old, I was aware of the shame I had for myself. No one ever told me to hate myself or abused me, but in second grade I wrote, "I hate Ben," and, "I want to hurt Ben," on an assignment. I drew a line through it, pretending like I didn't want my teacher to see it, but in truth, I wanted her to read It and help me, because I didn't know what to do with these hateful thoughts. My teacher came to me

concerned, but for whatever reason, no further help came my way.

In third grade I started having mysterious stomach aches and other physical symptoms which turned out to be rooted in anxiety and fear. In the summer before fourth grade, my grandfather died by suicide after a lifelong battle with depression. His suicide gave me a new option for what to do with my shame, one I didn't even know existed until then. By fifth grade I had regular thoughts of wanting to hurt myself and at times kill myself.

These early experiences created in me a quest to find the answers to the following two questions:

- Why did I hate myself so much so early in my life?
- Why couldn't I stop hating myself even when I knew better?

My adolescent and college years were full of going in and out of depressive cycles, suicidal fantasies, and a growing hatred of myself. Thank goodness for friendships, faith, counseling, and curiosity, as I was eventually able to turn my pain into a pursuit of understanding and healing, but it was rough.

The quest to answer my questions led me to a graduate program in marriage and family therapy, and while my graduate education was amazing, the most valuable part was the self-awareness I gained. As much as I wanted to become a therapist, I knew I was there to figure out what was going on with me, and if I ended up helping others, even better. Armed with this new knowledge and awareness of myself, though, I continued to struggle with self-worth, bouts of depression, and addictive behaviors, even as I helped others deal with theirs.

Wanting to feel more of what I knew was true about myself and others, though, I kept doing the hard work of exploring my inner self. Now, I can say I've been to the depths of despair and found a way out, but only after I stopped using self-abuse, shame, and hatred as tools for trying to motivate me or convince me to change. Stopping what wasn't working and addressing my problem of self-acceptance was what made all the difference.

I'm So Glad You're Here

Your journey awaits, and I want to be the first to welcome you. For now, I will be your guide. Since I have lived a lot of my life in self-hatred, I know what it's like from the inside. Not to brag, but I can, within a few thoughts, find my way back to dark places of hate and shame toward myself. At the same time, I know how to get myself out of those dark places and back into acceptance, and I want to help you learn to do the same. For some, the struggle for acceptance comes in more obvious forms like self-loathing, depression, anger, addictions, and anxiety. For others, it comes in more subtle expressions like pride, narcissistic behavior, people-pleasing, and perfectionism. Regardless of the form, it's all rooted in a contempt, hatred, or fear of one's self.

I would like to tell you I am completely over all experiences of self-hate and never, ever do it. However, I agreed to be completely honest with you and myself on this journey when I decided to write this book. I want you to know I still struggle with this at times and fall back into self-pity and hate. While writing this book I battled frequently with a voice in my head telling me how stupid I was for writing it, and I imagined readers like you rejecting me and my ideas. How embarrassing! I, the one who is supposed to be the expert, obsessed over the rejection of others while I wrote about acceptance. The irony was not lost on me. What I needed, and what got me through writing this, was my acceptance of me.

What this exposed was a valuable truth: As much as we'd like to think it's the acceptance of others we crave most, it's not. The acceptance we crave most is our own.

Think about it. What do we think we will feel when others accept us? What do we think the blessing and approval of a parent, partner, child, deity, or stranger on the internet is going to make us feel? Acceptable? Worthy? Adequate? Enough? Free?

We want others to accept us in order to give us permission to ultimately accept ourselves. However, if our acceptance is based on what others think of us, we are subject to how other people feel about us in the moment. This arrangement puts us in a tight spot, because just as easily as others can give us acceptance, they can also take it away. We need a way out of this precarious predicament, and acceptance of ourselves is the way.

When you decide to go on this journey, you are choosing to become the person who values, accepts, loves, and enjoys *you* the most. It's not about you never again struggling with acceptance and having a perfectly positive voice in your head at all times (that's impossible). This journey is about taking back the responsibility for your acceptance from anything or anyone outside of you.

This brings me to one more important truth I want you to know: Your journey is not about becoming more acceptable in any way. You will be no more acceptable by the end of this book, or at any other moment, than you are right now. This book is about the acceptance of yourself in the present and the final destination is being *liked* by you.

How You Might Benefit from Being Here

I don't know exactly why you picked up this book, but I am going to identify the types of people I imagine would come to this book, and how I believe reading it could be beneficial.

Perhaps you are desperately hurting and entrenched in self-hate and depression, and you aren't sure if there is any way out. If this is you, I imagine you are looking for something to get you out of your painful situation, some lifeline or hope, and like me at several points in my life, you may have even considered suicide as a way out. I welcome you to this book, and while it might not be everything you need to help you out of the pit you are in, I hope something in these pages will spark something or give you some new ideas for how to move forward. Maybe this can be a starting line for you.

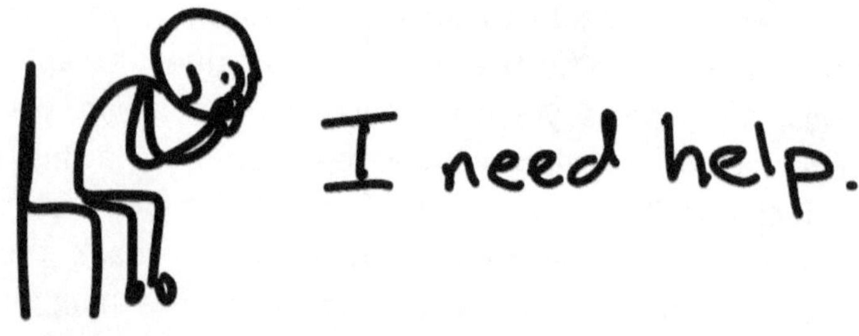

Do not substitute this book for professional help. If you are in a place of serious despair or are contemplating suicide, speak to a professional. You can start by calling the National Suicide Prevention Hotline at 1-800-273-8255, or in the US you can also dial 988.

Or maybe you are here because you find yourself being hateful towards yourself, don't want to be, and know that you deserve better. However, despite this knowledge, you keep regularly beating yourself up and feeling worthless. If this is you, you might have read other books, been to therapy, conferences, seminars, and find yourself frustrated because you are still struggling.

You have the knowledge, but something seems to keep getting in the way of you applying it consistently. This book offers you a number of different perspectives and possibilities for dealing with your problem so that you can finally break your cycle of self-hate and shame. Sometimes a shift in the way you see something is what you need to finally make the change you want.

Or maybe hate feels like too strong of a word for you, and although you wouldn't say you hate yourself, you don't really like yourself either. You are not really in a bad place, but something seems to be missing—like joy or fulfillment. I live in Oklahoma, and early in my life our state license plates read, "Oklahoma is OK." Not great, just OK. Yes, the great state of mediocrity. Maybe you live your life in this state (mediocrity, not Oklahoma), too. You know you could and should feel better about yourself, but you don't know how or where to begin. I look forward to sharing with you

and challenging you in this book to experience yourself and your true value in a richer, more meaningful way than you are right now. How great would it be to know you are good and feel it in your deepest self?

Maybe you picked this up out of curiosity and immediately thought of someone else, like a friend, child, parent, or co-worker who you want to help. If this is you, reading this will perhaps help you to better understand what is going on in their life. It will also help you to realize that you can't do their acceptance work for them, but you can keep loving and supporting them while they learn to do these things for themselves. If your first impulse is to give it to someone else, you should probably wait until you read it yourself.

Wherever you find yourself, I'm happy you are here. I hope you'll find useful concepts to apply in your life, as what's in here has saved my life. I wrote this to offer you new ways of interacting with yourself that have the power to transform your relationship with yourself and ultimately with others.

Why Self-Acceptance is So Radical

Why is self-acceptance even an issue? Shouldn't it be something very obvious and natural to do? I mean, despite many of us growing up seeing posters at school telling us how great we are just the way we are, and hearing messages about how we can be anything in the world we want to be, how can we still struggle so mightily with self-esteem and self-worth? What makes self-acceptance such a radical act? Let me address a few here.

Marketing. Most marketing messages follow this script, "You are not enough until you have ________." It's the most basic marketing formula, and you are inundated with it constantly. Your perceived lack within yourself is the market's gain. The more you believe something will make you better, or at least comparable to others, the more likely you are to buy it. This includes the vehicles you drive, the places you live, the clothes you wear, and even the latest self-help book or program you must have. I am not saying some of these things can't help you improve your life, but when you believe you are not enough without these things, you are not in a place to accept yourself as you are. Marketing typically tells you that you are not enough without whatever it is selling, and you might be tempted to believe it.

Conflicting messages. You might also be confused about your worth because of the conflicting messages in culture about it. We are a communal and tribal species as humans. In most of human history we depended on our connection to a tribe as our means of safety, protection, purpose, and meaning. Your acceptance used to be deeply rooted within that small tribe, and your value was directly tied to how you functioned within it. To go outside your tribe and make your own way was risky and could result in great shame to yourself and your family.

However, as we have continued to become more individualistic in most of the world, and especially in mainstream US culture, there is a huge emphasis on making your own way in life. This creates problems when what you need to grow as an individual (like autonomy and creativity) clashes with what the culture wants from you (like conformity and compliance). You and I sit in this tension to be ourselves, while at the same time fitting in with everyone else. We are also experiencing ever-increasing demands to not offend anyone and join the "correct" side, which has only seemed to divide us further both externally and internally.

Add this to the fact your tribe is now not a small group of people, but a massive network of global participants through things like social media. We are all watching each other and telling each other what to think, act, feel, and believe about everything, and we are becoming increasingly aware how no matter what we do or say, someone out there will inevitably not agree with us or perhaps even find us offensive. Self-acceptance is radical in this context because it requires you to accept yourself in a world that pressures you to do the impossible task of being accepted by everyone.

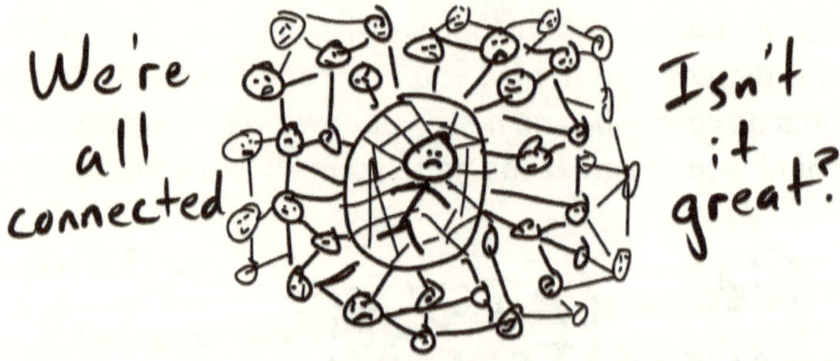

As a result, many of us attempt to get out of this bind by trying to live our lives without actually believing in anything, including ourselves. As a result, we tend to cancel and hold ourselves back before anyone else can find fault with us. It's impossible to accept ourselves when we are focused on being acceptable (or at least not un-acceptable) to everyone else.

Modeling. Poor self-acceptance could also be as simple as you not having a model of how to accept yourself. You initially learned how to see yourself by observing how others, especially your parents and/or caretakers, saw and interacted with themselves. By the way, your caretakers learned how to see themselves by how their caretakers saw and interacted with themselves. This is important because your view of yourself is shaped by generations before you, coming from people whose names you don't even know, but greatly influencing you and how you see yourself. You inherited these ways to see yourself without your input, and while your acceptance problem didn't start with you, it can end with you. If you make this change in how you accept yourself, you will influence generations to come. What could be better than passing on a legacy of self-acceptance?

Adaptation to your environment. Lastly, your struggles with acceptance may be due, in large part, to your past or present attempts to adapt to your environment. Adaptations are solutions for safety or survival in a particular environment. If you grew up in a family or environment where it was to your perceived or actual advantage to adapt by devaluing or denying yourself for the sake of the family or for safety (like avoiding abuse or criticism), then this adaptation became your way of operating in the world. What happened, though, is once you got out of that environment, you continued to apply the adaptive behavior to your new environments. One way to know if you are doing this is to look at areas of life where your reactions to something seem way out of proportion to what triggered it. For example, getting extremely angry when your partner or teenager points out something you did that bothered them screams adaptation.

Children with an insecure, unhealthy parent often adapted by trying to become a parent to their parent. Children who adapted this way were attempting to keep their parent emotionally regulated, or at least not too unregulated, in order to avoid the parent either going off on them physically or emotionally, or from the parent withdrawing love or neglecting them. Children in this situation developed a high sensitivity not only to the emotions of their parents, but to everything around them as they were constantly scanning for something that felt off. To become more sensitive to their environment, however, these children learned to be less sensitive, or not sensitive at all, to their own feelings and needs.

This is one of the most damaging adaptations a child can make because the child will ultimately fail at keeping the parent regulated, leading to the child feeling defeated and inadequate. Even if the child does "succeed," it comes at the cost of the child's own development and growth, and results in the child continuing to carry the responsibility for the parent into adulthood. Another significant price paid is the child's loss of a sense of worth and value outside of what one can do or be for others, and this often carries on into adulthood.

Were you, or do you remember, the class clown? The class clown role is also an adaptation. In this case, a person is trying to avoid feeling insecure about one's place in the class, either socially or academically, and is acting out in order to hide that insecurity. I remember a kid at school who adapted to his insecurity about his appearance by making fun of himself and putting himself down in front of others. He also joined others in teasing himself so they would accept him. While this may have gained him friends, it kept him in his insecurity and self-contempt.

Adaptations, like being the class clown, often result in feelings of low self-worth. Personally, I adapted in my family by devaluing my needs and myself for the sake of the family. I didn't want to add any problems or stress, especially to my mother, and wanted to keep peace. This adaptation, while it seemed helpful to me at ten years old, came at the cost of seeing myself as less important than everyone else. To this day, I still feel seduced into trying to adapt like this in my family and other groups. Fortunately, through my personal journey of discovery, I now have a greater ability to recognize this former adaptation, and I avoid it the best I can.

While all these factors, and certainly others, contribute to the massive acceptance problem we have in the world, they do not exempt us from the need of taking responsibility for our own acceptance. At some point we all need to realize that regardless of what happened in our childhoods or how we are manipulated by media and marketing messages, as adults we are responsible for our lives moving forward and are capable of making things different. I am calling you to the radical act of taking the responsibility for your acceptance, regardless of what you've experienced thus far in your life.

Safe-Hate is Being Used as a Solution to a Problem

Here's a major point, and I will yell it from the rooftops: You don't have a self-hate problem, you have a problem of using self-hate as a solution. The root problem is not, has not, and never will be self-hate. Self-hate has been a way of dealing with your lack of self-acceptance. If you accepted yourself you would not have a reason to be self-hating. Continuing to apply self-hate in your life is like saying, "Well, since I don't feel acceptable, I'll hate myself, because if I hate myself enough maybe the hate will motivate me to do something to get accepted by others."

Your lack of acceptance is the problem and the solution is acceptance. Continuing to put in you a sense of lack is something marketers and narcissists do to keep you buying their products and responding to their demands. This book focuses on addressing a self-acceptance problem so that any self-hating behaviors that you might have will cease to make sense as a solution.

An Introduction to the Map and the Destination

The self-acceptance pyramid is the map for your journey to a place of ultimate acceptance of yourself: *Liked*. Each level is a form of acceptance in itself and builds on the one before it. The work you do in each level creates momentum to move into the next one as you answer the following questions:

- How do I become more tolerant of myself?
- How do I better appreciate myself?
- How do I reconcile myself to myself?
- How do I love myself?
- How do I like myself?

All these levels are powerful and each is transformative in its own way.

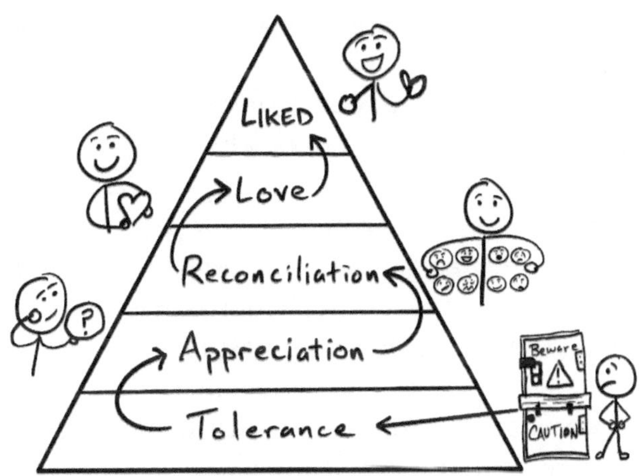

For instance, the first level of *tolerance* can be the difference for some people between life and death, because they finally open up to something they thought they had to destroy. A simple, but often difficult step of being tolerant toward something creates an opportunity to change your relationship to it. When you have little or no tolerance for yourself, you don't always see how fragile you've become, but when you begin to be tolerant of yourself, even in little ways, you start to realize how vital it is.

The second level is *appreciation* because once you become more tolerant of yourself, you are able to turn your attention to finding value both in yourself and whatever you experience. You do this by becoming more curious and less judgmental. We'll look at how to use curiosity to open you up to greater appreciation, because curiosity allows you to find more value in what is already in your life.

After this, the journey brings you to *reconciliation*, where you will learn how to rejoin and reconnect yourself to yourself. This results in a greater sense of wholeness and integrity because you embrace who you are as a whole person. We'll explore the different postures of reconciliation that you can take in order to increase your ability to more fully experience wholeness.

Love is the next move on your journey. Love is the unrelenting commitment and care of yourself. This level is about being dedicated to your growth by creating an environment where you can flourish. Love is where you act in accordance with what is best for you.

Liked sits at the top of the pyramid. It's the highest level because it is the experience of the acceptance *and* enjoyment of yourself. I don't know of any greater acceptance than liking who you are. At this level you give yourself the permission to unashamedly be who you are by no longer trying to be anyone else. When you are here you live life from acceptance rather than for acceptance.

5 Last Instructions Before Take Off

Feel free to move about the cabin after you get comfortable. Take time to read and work through the levels as they are laid out. The levels build on each other, and you will be better off going through them sequentially. Once you go through them and have a good feel for them, then you can go back and explore.

Reach out for help if you need it. While this book is about self-acceptance, don't hesitate to get support from others. This journey might take you to some deep places inside yourself and bring up some uncomfortable emotions. If it feels like too much, put the book down and reach out for help. No one can do the work for you, but they may be able to walk alongside you as you do it, providing support and a sense of safety. This includes finding a therapist or coach skilled in guiding people through their inner work and processes.

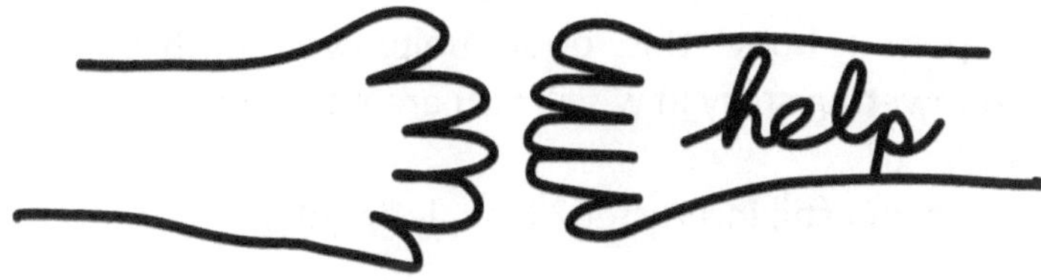

Expect turbulence, because it means you're bumping up against your stuff. Turbulence in an airplane means the wings are bumping into the air, which is a really good thing if you think about it, because it means there is air to bump against and keep you in the sky. This book will likely cause you to bump up against both your old and current thoughts, beliefs, emotions, and ways of being. You may have to wrestle with yourself in order to come up with new understandings for your life. Remember that discomfort is a key ingredient in change because we don't tend to change when we're comfortable. If it gets too bumpy, you can always reach out for help.

Turn the knowledge you gain into action. "There's a difference between knowing the path and walking the path," explained Morpheus to Neo in *The Matrix*. Just as a hiking map is a representation of the hike and not the hike itself, this book can only show you the path. If you only read this book and don't take any action in your life, you'll wind up with more information, but not much else (except maybe more frustration and anxiety!). To grow you must apply the knowledge and put it into action.

The most important story you can hear is the one you tell yourself about yourself. No story matters more than the one you tell yourself. This book is about helping you to tell a different story to yourself in which you are worthy, valuable, and acceptable just as you are *right now*. We treat ourselves according to the stories we tell ourselves about who we are and what we deserve. Change your story and there's no telling what might happen. I hope this book helps you embrace an empowering story in which you are not only acceptable but *liked!*

Are you still interested? If so, let's get started!

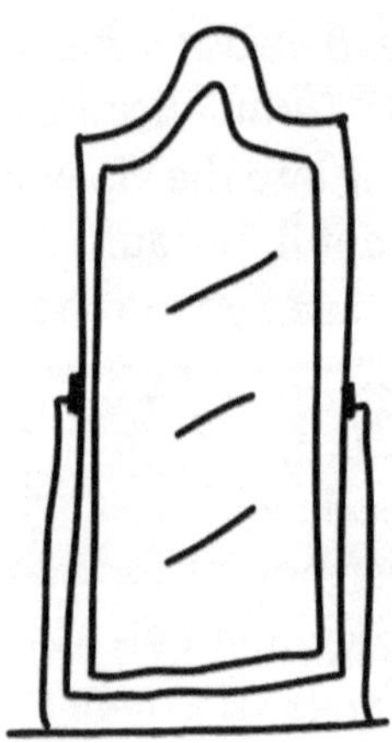

2

Tolerance

Tolerance is an openness to what is

Before We Can Talk about Tolerance

Tolerance is the starting point of self-acceptance and sits at the base of the pyramid because it supports all the rest. In the absence of tolerance, your life is starving for acceptance, but as soon as you can find even the smallest amount of tolerance, you begin the journey toward acceptance. In fact, a little tolerance can be the difference between love or hate, a fight or an embrace, and even life or death. To understand tolerance we first need to understand intolerance.

Intolerance is being closed off and unaccepting of something. When you do not believe you can exist peacefully as long as a certain feeling, pain, or situation also exists in your life, you are being intolerant. This puts you at higher risk for doing something drastic to yourself, from one extreme of self-hate, such as devaluing, debasing, or rejecting yourself, to the other extreme of serious depression, self-harm, and even suicide. This explains why self-hate, in all of its forms, happens across all cultures, demographics, social-economic statuses, and ages. Intolerance has less to do with external or internal conditions and more to do with our internal, closed off responses to those conditions.

Intolerance keeps you as a prisoner behind a door that you've locked, waiting for your sentence to end. Tolerance ends your sentence instantly and gives you the freedom to both unlock and open the door. This might not be easy to wrap your head around right now, but it is where every 12-step recovery program starts: "We admitted we were powerless over _________." Now that we can agree to leave intolerance behind, we can explore the power of tolerance.

Tolerance is an Openness to What is

Tolerance is the first step into acceptance because it opens you up to your condition right now, without having to change a thing. It is an openness to yourself and your behaviors, beliefs, values, and treatment toward yourself and others, both past and present. It's not a blanket approval of all those things, but it is first and foremost an open acknowledgment of all of them. Knowing this can help you avoid the confusion of thinking tolerance, and by extension, acceptance, only happens when you are good enough or deserving enough for it— tolerance is a state of being, not an earned status.

Think about tolerance as moving from a place of contempt for yourself to a place of contemplation of yourself. Instead of shaming yourself you are seeking out yourself with a more open mind. As you increase tolerance, you'll increase your ability to engage with yourself and whatever you are experiencing.

Tolerance is not about being dismissive or ignorant of the undesirable actions you are doing or have done. It is about being open to yourself and what you've done so that you can take purposeful and responsible action in your life. Let's look at how this plays out.

Tolerance Increases Your Capacity for Responsibility

Take the word responsibility apart and you get the words "response" and "ability," and it literally means the ability to respond. The more ability you have to respond to something rationally and purposefully, the more capacity you have for responsibility. Responsibility for yourself is unavoidable, you can't escape it. You can try to ignore it or give it away to others, but it will always come back to you. Whatever comes into your life becomes your responsibility, because you have to decide what you are going to do with it and how you are going to respond to it. You are not responsible for other's actions towards you, of course, only your response.

Tolerance increases your capacity to take responsibility for your life and your choices by becoming more open to them. While tolerance does not excuse or condone harming yourself or others, it does mean being tolerant of yourself even if you did. Again, this is not as a way of making what you did okay or denying any harm it caused, but to open you up to an understanding of what you did and why you did it, so that you can take greater responsibility for

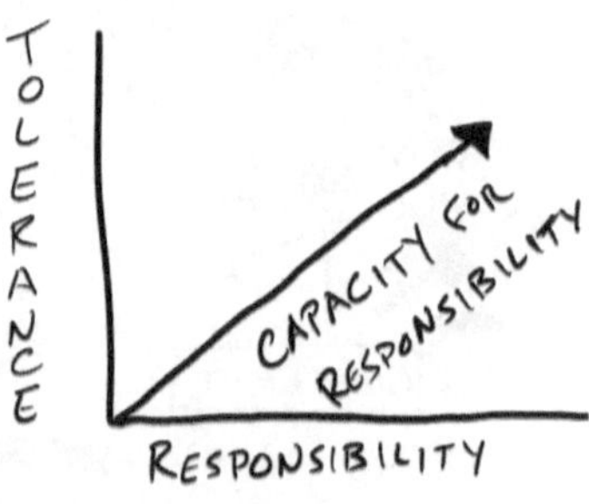

it. Tolerance that excuses maltreatment of others isn't true tolerance, it's more like entitlement (acting like "you made me do it"), and only increases irresponsibility. For instance, telling others that they have to listen to you regardless of how you are talking to them is not being tolerant, it's being entitled. Tolerance would be asking someone to have a conversation with you and then being willing to engage in dialogue with an openness to both sides. Tolerance focuses on responsibility, while entitlement focuses on rights.

Tolerance Allows You to Simply Encounter Something

I wonder how many destructive things have happened in the world because people believed they could not or should not have a certain inclination, feeling, or thought. Whether from cultural, religious, or family programming, struggles with mental illness, past trauma, or some unknown origin, they felt a strong prohibition about something, and yet, no matter what, they couldn't stop the thought, feeling, or behavior.

Unfortunately, though, oftentimes out of shame or fear of an inability to control it, they didn't seek any help or guidance. Unable to work through it outwardly they became increasingly consumed and condemned by it inwardly. Many eating disorders, emotional disorders, psychiatric disorders, and addictions share this common root of self-condemnation. At the most extreme ends people have made tragic decisions to end their lives or other's lives because of their inability to control what was happening on the inside, which led them to destroy the object of their prohibition on the outside.

Think about it in your own life—what have you been told to not think, feel, doubt, or even consider? What were your prohibitions, and how have you adapted to them? One thing I know for sure is being told not to think or feel something did not actually stop you from thinking or feeling it.

When you aren't open to something occurring inside you, you close yourself off to the very understanding that could ultimately increase your capacity to take responsibility. If you can't or shouldn't have certain thoughts about race, gender, sexuality, religion, money, beauty, your family, etc., then you are stuck either seeing yourself as intolerable, or stuck trying to convince yourself that your thoughts and feelings are correct and need to be strongly defended. However, if you are open to engaging those thoughts, then you increase your capacity to respond to them by working through them, challenging them, researching them, deciding what you really believe, or simply allowing them to be there without your resistance.

You cannot wait to unlock the door to yourself until you have all the "right" thoughts and feelings, do all the "right" things, or have your life all cleaned up, because that's impossible (you won't ever have it all "right"). Trying to do so would only reinforce the false belief that you can earn your acceptance.

Trying to change yourself before being tolerant of yourself would be like giving a child or teenager the label of "lazy" or "ungrateful" and then foolishly expecting them to try to prove you wrong, rather than prove your label of them right. Your label of them is the expectation, no matter what else you say. Likewise, without tolerance you will continue to wear the labels "intolerable" and "unacceptable" and do the things consistent with those labels. Through tolerance you can encounter yourself as one who is "acceptable" and "worthy," opening you up to a vast new set of options in your life consistent with those labels.

Tolerance is the first essential step to increasing your capacity for responsibility. When you stop judging yourself for your experiences and behaviors and increasingly become tolerant of yourself then you will realize a new power to take responsible action in your life.

You Belong at the Table

One way to think of tolerance is to imagine what you do when there is a family member you can't stand, but you know you have to see them for three hours when they come over for a family event, like Thanksgiving or Christmas dinner. The key to handling it well is to find a reason they belong at the table. It could be as simple as they are related to others at the table, or they were invited by the host, or they are a human like you who deserves the dignity of being there despite past transgressions.

If you still need a way to make it survivable you can always remind yourself of something kind the person did one time, or think of what they mean to others at the table. You might have to dig deep, but you can probably find something.

Tolerance for yourself is realizing you belong at the table of your life regardless of your past actions or any present conditions. It means seeing yourself as valuable as anyone else. You belong because you exist and your existence is the only invitation that matters. Once you've established your belongingness, you can further reinforce it by seeing the good in you.

This is About Tolerance for You, Not Others

I want to make clear I am not talking about finding ways to be tolerant of people who have done terrible things to you. *This is not about tolerance for other people, it's about tolerance for you.*

What practicing tolerance *for yourself* allows you to do is to encounter difficult people and people who have harmed you with a greater tolerance of what *you* are feeling and experiencing about or because of them. Doing this keeps you open to what you are feeling and increases your capacity to respond. If you feel hate, you can be open to feeling it. If you feel a strange attraction to a person, you can pay attention to it. If you feel any conflicting feelings within yourself then you can be tolerant of those, too.

If you aren't free to have the feelings you are having, then the problem is not the feelings, but that you are not yet free. Once free you can gain a greater ability to respond to your feelings in new ways.

When You're Free to Feel, You're Free to Heal

Mark, a man I worked with, was filled with deep hate for his parents and what they had put him through, especially in his younger years. When he was nine, they had an ugly divorce, but he stayed loyal to both of them. He covered up his mother's drinking and took care of her, and he took care of his father by becoming a tough and self-sufficient man that didn't need any help. Like many children who became a parent to one or both of their parents, he grew to deeply resent the backwardness of this relationship.

As much as he hated them, he had a strong conviction it was not okay to hate them. He wasn't free to feel that hate and he was in agony over to the point of contemplating suicide.

Mark, through a deeply emotional process and experience, finally became tolerant of his hate. The years of denial and suppressed feelings that he locked in his body finally released. This began a dramatic change in his life and his relationship with himself, and consequently allowed him to determine the relationship he wanted with his parents, without having to deny himself or his feelings anymore. Free to feel, free to heal.

Have you been here before or are you here now—stuck with a feeling you don't think is okay to have, but feeling helpless to do anything about it? Tolerance is a way out.

Start with Something You Have in Common...with Yourself

If you imagine that tolerance only happens when you love yourself and are happy with yourself, I encourage you to re-evaluate this belief. Tolerance happens the moment you open yourself up to something.

I realized the power of tolerance when I was turning out of a parking lot and someone completely cut me off. I was irate, debating the use of one of my digits, but then I noticed the offending car was the same make and model as mine. Instantly, I found myself tolerant simply because I drove the same kind of car as the offender. I thought, "We're in this together," and calmed down. It was so ridiculous. The only difference in my reaction came down to finding one thing I had in common with the other driver.

We do this all the time if we're honest. We become more tolerant because someone looks like us, wears the same kind of shoes, is a fan of the same football team, or smiles at us and says a kind word. One simple connection with someone and we are more tolerant. Surely you can find something like this in yourself. I mean, how many things do you have in common with yourself? And you just have to find one.

Find something you can connect to in or about yourself—your desire to feel better, your intelligence, your humor, your taste in shoes, your humanness, your smile, etc. By doing this you unlock the acceptance door and are one step closer to cracking it open.

Slowly Increase Your Capacity for Discomfort

Once you unlock the door, keep it unlocked so you can continue to see that little sliver of light you get when you loosen the locks but haven't opened it yet. In doing this you are increasing your capacity for discomfort and your ability to be open. At this point tolerance is about simply not locking the door again. When you feel like locking the door because something feels uncomfortable, practice keeping it unlocked. Your capacity for discomfort will grow the more you do this, and just like a muscle gets stronger when you consistently work it out, you'll increase your ability to remain open to difficult things.

A simple way to start practicing this is to notice a feeling you are having, and then give the feeling a name. Shame. Fear. Anxiety. Discomfort. Hatred. Happy. Sexy. After you name the feeling, imagine yourself sitting with it, and do the following:

Avoid avoiding it. Resist the urge to run from it or block it out. Don't run or close yourself off to it.

Give it a number. Since you've already started this by naming it, give it a number. On a 0-10 scale of intensity, with zero being, "Meh, no biggie," to ten being, "I feel like I am about to explode," ask yourself how intense it feels.

Consciously reflect on it. Think about why it's there. Did something trigger it? Does it remind you of something? Does it seem like the feeling it is creating is proportionate to what caused it? What are your judgments of it?

Try it right now if you are able. Think about a time you did something you are not proud of or when you made a mistake. Now, notice the feeling coming up and name it. Notice how you experience this feeling in your body. Also, notice any attempt to avoid it. Give it a number from 1-10, representing how intense the feeling is. Finally, reflect on your experience of it.

That's all you need to do with it. You don't have to solve it or beat yourself up about it, just observe it and refuse to simply avoid it. This is how you practice building up your capacity for tolerance, even if slowly.

If this is too difficult, painful, or overwhelming, try doing it with something less triggering for you, but don't force it, and if you need to then seek help from a professional (therapist, coach, yoga or meditation teacher, etc.) to help you increase your tolerance for discomfort.

Open the Door...Slowly

After you develop a greater ability to keep the door unlocked with the first two steps, work on opening the door to yourself a little wider. If you're like me, you have some stories in your past where you threw the door open to something or someone way too fast, realized it was too much, and locked the door, and maybe even added a new lock.

I did this in college in front of a class of about 50 peers. I shared some details about a personal past relationship, and right after the words left my mouth, I felt a heavy weight of shame. I locked the door back for a while after that because I believed I marked myself as a poor relationship choice forever. That wasn't true, of course, but it sure felt like it at the time.

Opening the door slowly is like hearing a knock on your front door. Instead of throwing the door wide open, you peer through the peephole to see who it is. Then, you unlock and open the door based on how comfortable you are with the person. The more comfortable you are, the more you can open the door.

For instance, if you struggle with something like anger, depression, or anxiety, open the door enough to get a little better understanding of it, rather than throwing it open right away. As you get to know and understand it, you will find that you get more comfortable. You can do this with anything you experience like a thought, emotion, or behavior.

What if You Can't Find Anything to Tolerate about Yourself?

You may be so masterful at intolerance or self-hate after years of practice that it's become second nature to see only the negative in you and your situations. I suggest breaking this habit with new strategies, because if you don't change what you're doing, you won't be able to make any progress. The following are a few ways to move from intolerance to tolerance:

See and talk to yourself like you would to a friend. Unless you are highly judgmental of all your friends and secretly despise them and see the worst in them, this strategy can help. Try seeing yourself like a good friend, and then talk to yourself like you would talk to them. Most of us would not say to a friend, "You stupid idiot, why can't you get anything right?" (Note: If you do speak to your friends like this, please stop if you want to continue having friends). Instead, you probably say things like, "Don't be so hard on yourself, things just didn't turn out like you wanted. You are a good person." Your experience of life will be better when you talk to yourself this way.

Why is it that we see the best in our friends and the worst in ourselves? I think it's largely because we want to believe about ourselves what we say to others. For instance, we want to believe we don't have to be perfect and deserve grace rather than punishment when we fall short of an expectation. We want to believe we are worthy of respect even when we make mistakes. But this is where it can get twisted up.

We might believe we are being humble by seeing ourselves as lower and less worthy than others, but aren't we doing the opposite? By giving ourselves harsh judgment instead of grace, we're telling ourselves we are better than those who need grace and kindness. Recognizing this twist was a game-changer for me because 1) I really didn't like to think of myself as superior to others, and 2) when I stopped trying to be perfect to be acceptable, I could let myself be perfectly human. Understand this can do the same thing for you.

When you see yourself like you see your friends, you are accepting that you are human and deserve what everyone else does, which keeps you from thinking that you are any worse (or better) than anyone else.

Take someone else's word for it. Whether or not you think you are good or tolerable, someone out there thinks differently. Maybe it's a family member like your partner, parent, or grandparent who sees you as good. It might be a friend or a trusted person in your life like a mentor, pastor, therapist, coach, or teacher. Of course, you can always seemingly find a reason to discount their beliefs because they "have to" see you like this, but even if you can't see it yourself, you should trust that others can from their vantage point.

This is mainly to help you in the beginning as you are developing tolerance. As you get better at tolerance for yourself you'll have less of a need to derive it from others. The goal is not to reject their tolerance, but to be free of *depending* on it.

Find a community that values you. If you are in a religious or spiritual community, I hope you are part of one where you feel valued and understood. A community like this can be a good place to experience and learn about tolerance. If it is not a place where you hear positive messages about you or if it leaves you feeling guilty and shameful, it may help to take a step back and evaluate if it is a place where you need to be. I know at times in my past, I received religious messages to be scared and ashamed of myself instead of tolerant and accepting. A pastor or priest or spiritual leader in the community may be able to help you make sense of this, but if not, it's okay to look somewhere else. A good leader, whether religious or secular (because this certainly does not apply only to religious leaders), will listen to you and come alongside you, not shame you or push you to blindly adopt a set of beliefs.

Religious groups are not the only place to find communal support. Support groups, local community groups, and online groups can offer places where you can find support. It requires discretion with any group to see if they are a good fit for you. At the very least, it should be a place respectful of your autonomy, value system, and personhood, without telling you what you should think, feel, or do without your permission. Don't stay somewhere with little respect for individuals and their right to run their own lives.

Take my word for it. I hope you can take my word for it. I believe in the goodness of you. You are good even if your behaviors have not always been good. You are good even if you can't see it, and you are not bad if you can't see it. You are valuable, despite what anyone might have told you.

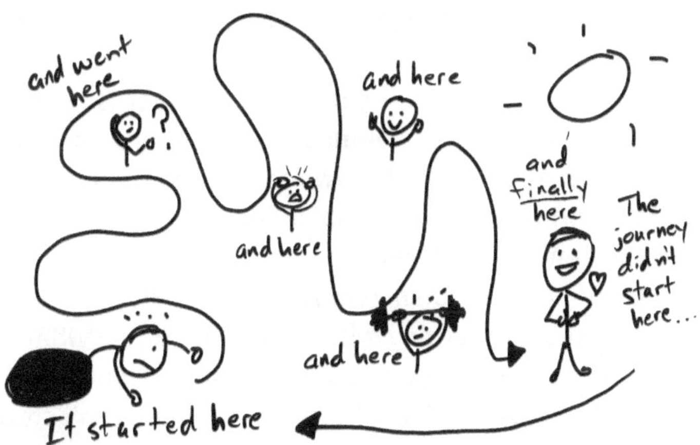

I've been in places of total despair and serious contemplation of suicide, having to fight to see anything good about myself. In those places I scoffed at people trying to tell me I was good, so I understand if this offends you or seems ridiculous. I can't do this journey for you, but I can tell you it was worth it for me and that

I found a way out. I had to trust others in my life who believed in my value when I didn't. I had to learn to see myself like I do my friends. I learned it's more important to believe the truth about me more than the feelings I had about me.

I didn't start my journey out by a lightning strike of tolerance, but by slowly becoming more tolerant of myself. To expect you to go from self-loathing to tolerance in a moment is to set you up for failure. It takes time and effort.

Three Fears Blocking Openness

Some people are ready to unlock the door and walk straight through, but for those of you who are saying, "Yes, I want to be more open toward myself, but I can't seem to make it happen," it will help to understand the following fears. Each of these fears keeps you from unlocking the door and being open to what is on the other side. It is in no way negative or wrong to have these fears as they are hardwired into us for survival, not to mention that you would not be having these fears if you weren't facing them.

Fear of the unknown removes choice. It is difficult to be open to something when you don't know what it means or will mean to you. You fear what you don't know, and this puts you in a bind, because you often can't stop fearing something until you know what it is and whether or not you need to fear it. It's the proverbial monster in the closet—you will fear it until you know what it is. When you choose to keep something unknown you are removing the choice to know it.

I had a friend in college who wouldn't check his grades at the end of a semester for weeks after they were posted. He feared the unknown, which were his actual grades, and also how he was going to feel when he saw them. When he finally looked at them, he was always relieved, not because they were always good, but because he didn't have to live in fear of them anymore. Still, he played this game every semester and removed his choice to face his emotions until he stopped avoiding the unknown.

Fear of punishment removes agency. People who experience a heightened fear of punishment often grew up in environments where compliance and conformity were highly valued and enforced. Falling short of what was expected meant punishment through force or neglect, physically, emotionally and/or verbally. As a result, they found ways to avoid being punished by falling in line or at least looking like they did to the people who might punish them. Does this describe your experience at all?

If so, as an adult, you might find yourself fearing that if you talk about something or express an opinion, you will be punished in some way. This leaves you feeling like you have little choice in your life but to comply or stay quiet. Few things cause more resentment than feeling like you can't express something without pushback or punishment.

The problem here is the choices you are making to avoid punishment (staying quiet, avoiding conflict, etc.) keep you from working through or expressing something important. It's hard to feel you have agency in life when you are anticipating a painful conclusion from your actions.

If you are in a situation where you are routinely punished, physically, emotionally, or verbally, by someone else for any reason, you need to reach out for help, because you are in an abusive situation. Depending on the kind of abuse and level of it, the help you need will vary. One place to start is the National Domestic Violence Hotline by phone at 1-800-799-7233, and online at thehotline.org. They can give you guidance, as well as any local agencies like the Department of Human Services in the US.

Fear of being overwhelmed removes possibility. Do you ever fear you'll be overwhelmed by whatever you are holding inside? Are you afraid you will lose control, fall apart, or be unable to stop it from taking over? The fear of being overwhelmed is enough to keep many people from even *approaching* something uncomfortable.

In my life this looked like being so afraid of being overwhelmed by my sadness, that I shut it out and covered it up with humor and other coping mechanisms, like alcohol, watching movies, and helping others. But, as it turned out for me (and turns out for everybody eventually) avoidance only leads to more avoidance and more coping behaviors. It's one never-ending tornado until you get out of it.

If you fear being overcome by a feeling, you will try hard to keep under control no matter what, often white-knuckling it through situations, dangerously teetering on the edge of completely losing it. Predictably, something will finally tip the scales and chances are you will lose it and feel completely out of control to stop it, and you will end up reacting at a level much higher than when you first felt it.

The same scenario plays out if you are intensely afraid of feeling lonely, rejected, or separate from others. This could lead to you holding back any opinions, staying in terrible relationships, not putting up healthy boundaries, and never standing up for yourself—essentially rejecting yourself. What you are afraid of (like feeling rejected) ends up being exactly what you actually feel.

As long as you are doing more to avoid something than you are to address it, you're only reinforcing the power of the thing you are avoiding, and you will get more of the thing you fear. Once you face it, then you can turn your energy and focus toward dealing with it.

When you address these fears you are better able to keep the door open to what you need to face. Your increased tolerance will pay you dividends over time as long as you continue to apply it.

Don't Wait Until You are "Good Enough" Before You Become Tolerant

You might have a list without even knowing it. It is a list of who you must please or what you must possess before you can be tolerant of yourself. Your list fills in the blank of "I will be tolerant of myself when _____________." Below are some examples:

- I am smart enough
- I make a certain salary or have a certain title
- I am the perfect spouse
- I don't make mistakes anymore
- My parents tell me I'm good enough
- I weigh 5/10/20/150 less pounds
- My kids/spouse/parents/boss are happy with me
- I win a reality TV show
- I'm not depressed anymore
- I stop having negative thoughts
- I eat appropriate amounts of food
- I know why I do all the things I do

You might think that achieving any of these might make you feel more tolerable towards yourself, but none of them will make you any more acceptable. In fact, tolerance of yourself before or without these kinds of things is the whole point. If this was not true then acceptance would always be both conditional and something that could be earned.

You Need to Tell Yourself When it's Enough with the Self-Hate

Jim spent much of his life with feelings of low self-worth. Now in his sixties, Jim had grown quite accustomed to mentally abusing himself every night when he went to bed. He would second guess his past behaviors, resent himself, put himself down, and just lie there in self-contempt.

I enjoyed talking with Jim because he was honest and funny, but also had a self-disparaging Rodney Dangerfield-esque humor towards himself. Making fun of ourselves can be an important skill to have when we are playfully accepting our humanity and fallibility, but when it becomes a way to shame ourselves or hold ourselves in contempt, it crosses the line into being unhealthy and damaging. Jim had crossed this line. It wasn't funny anymore because it was shame, and it needed to stop.

We talked about what he could do about his shaming habit because it clearly wasn't helping him improve. He decided when he started down the sad road of regret and self-abuse at night that he would catch himself and say, "Jim, that's enough. It's not helping." He did this consistently until it broke up his pattern and he was able to avoid excessive self-shame. He stopped lying in a bed of contempt and started sleeping more.

If you use this strategy, I recommend referring to yourself in the third person as it creates some distance. It's like having a coach say, "Thompson, cut it out!" If shame or self-deprecation actually worked in helping us improve our lives, it would have worked by now, so it's time to stop.

Developing Toddlerance

Whether or not you've parented a toddler, you've probably been held hostage by one before—in an airplane, restaurant, family gathering, funeral, or any other place where you could not easily escape. Before you knew it, you became a witness, and maybe victim, to an uncontrollable fit with screaming, wailing, and defiant behavior.

The best way to prepare yourself for this situation is to develop what I call *toddlerance*, which is defined as the ability to be tolerant of a toddler without harming the toddler or becoming a toddler yourself. It's no easy feat! When lacking in toddlerance, people tend to either act like a toddler along with the toddler, or the opposite, become so detached that they are seemingly unaffected in any way by the drama (while everyone around them suffers).

The key is to find a healthy middle where you can (1) increase your tolerance, (2) avoid losing your wits or completely detaching, and (3) stay connected in a helpful way. This is toddlerance.

I bring this up because you need to learn how to stay connected to yourself when you experience something that feels uncomfortable or intolerable. If you have a toddler or remember being a toddler, you know a toddler feels out of control and not responsible for the experience. A toddler's brain simply does not have the wiring or ability to see this, but it's a good thing you are now a grown-up with an adult brain and can see through the emotional facade—or at least you can learn to. You have to get back into a place of tolerance so you can take responsibility for yourself and realize what felt so threatening and powerful before is disarmed by your ability to stay connected.

Without Toddlerance We're Stuck with Shaming Ourselves

Perhaps like me, you've witnessed "other" parents having little tolerance for their toddlers and being extremely impatient with them. It's like we forget they are small humans in a big world full of experiences they don't understand. We find ourselves saying things like: "How dare you throw a fit! You've got it easy, so stop complaining. Be better than that! Get it together! Forget your brain has not yet developed and you are almost completely run by emotion and external events, just start behaving…now! Why can't you listen to me when I am yelling at you?"

Worse, I've heard parents call their toddlers names, scorn them, and neglect them. It's not pretty, but it happens, and if it happened to you as a child, I hope you have come to realize your parents said these things about you out of their own immaturity, and not because what they said was true.

When you treat children with this type of intolerance, they do not learn to correct their behavior, they learn to see themselves according to the words and actions applied to them. They learn shame and fear rather than value and belonging. As they grow up, some unfortunately become experts at punishing themselves and others. A parent's voice becomes their own voice, and they no longer hear the difference. In therapy they often have to learn how to differentiate their voice from their parent's voice.

Not a pretty picture, is it? And yet this is the same intolerance we often give ourselves as adults. We beat ourselves up over mistakes or forget to be kind. We call ourselves names, hoping by shaming ourselves we will improve our behavior, but only end up with more shame. Maybe you even have a special name reserved for when you really mess up. My go to in the past was Stupid Idiot (in its mildest form).

If we wouldn't or shouldn't treat children like this, why would we treat ourselves this way?

You Treat Yourself and Others According to Your Stories about Them

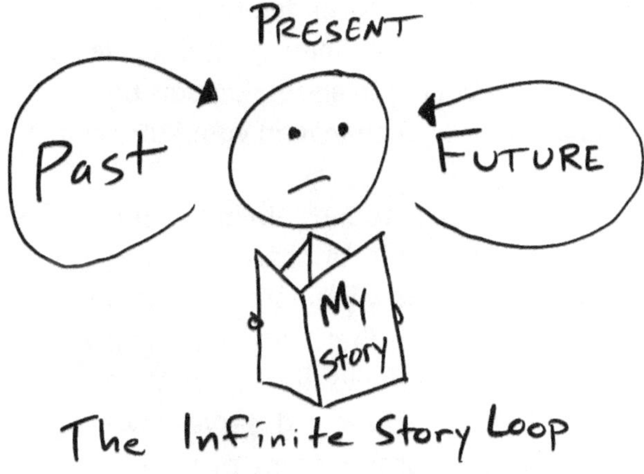

You only treat a toddler (or anyone for that matter) according to the stories that you tell about them. If you tell stories about how toddlers are stupid, evil, manipulative, or sent here to torture you for how you treated your parents, you will respond in negative, hurtful ways. If you see them as children learning to make sense of their place and their power and as deserving of respect and patience, you are more likely to treat them well.

Likewise, you only treat yourself according to the stories that you tell yourself. If you tell stories about how you are unlovable, unacceptable, and/or shameful, my guess (and experience) is you will treat yourself horribly.

On the other hand, if you tell stories about yourself being lovable, good, and worthy of respect, you will treat yourself in a completely different way. You will be more forgiving and open to receiving love from both yourself and others. You will treat yourself like you would treat anyone else you see as good and worthy.

When you understand that it is the stories you tell that you are fulfilling in your life, then you can address those stories and seek to understand them. Tolerance involves not only being open to the stories you tell yourself or have been told about yourself, but also being open to new stories. A change in your story can change your life.

I know this may sound obvious, but it's worth examining, because you can learn a lot about yourself by simply looking at how you interact with yourself and asking the question, "What story am I believing about myself in order to treat myself this way?"

"I guess I don't believe I deserve anything good," answered Steve, a former client of mine when asked this. Despite having a successful business, a beautiful family he loved, and the life he dreamed of as a child, he believed he was undeserving of good things. However, he did the work of changing the stories he told himself. His old stories died hard (as they tend to do), but over time his new story became, "I am a good person. I can have good things in my life, and don't have to feel guilty for being successful." Most importantly, he began to live out his new stories.

You Tolerate Yourself as a Grownup Like You Were Tolerated Growing Up

It is important to answer the question, "How can I be more tolerant of myself?" However, I want to go one step back in your life and ask the question, "How were you tolerated as a child?" I'm convinced by the research I've seen and years of observation that how you were tolerated as a child is a strong indicator of how you tend to tolerate yourself now.

What does this mean for you? It could be a justification for continuing to think and behave the way you do toward yourself because you didn't cause it. It's seductive and easy to get stuck here because it relieves you of responsibility. It could also (and I hope this is the case for you) lead you to be more responsible for yourself and your tolerance because you consciously choose to tolerate yourself rather than unconsciously defaulting to how you learned to be tolerant (or intolerant) of yourself.

Since young children do not yet have a strong sense of self, they are at the mercy of how others react to them to teach them who they are. They are formed intentionally or unintentionally to see themselves as good or bad, worthy or unworthy, a child or a menace. Parents, other caregivers, and siblings were the primary teachers of this, and as the child grows up, outside influences carry more weight as well.

The most outwardly and inwardly judgmental people I know were not tolerated well as children, meaning their growth and increasing individuality were experienced as a threat to be resisted or rejected in their family. They were criticized when they acted out, told they needed to be better family members, and punished when they departed from the family's expectations.

On the other hand, if you were tolerated well by your parents and others, you learned that it's okay to be you and to grow and to explore the world. You learned that acting out did not mean you were bad, and as a result you are more likely to be tolerant of yourself as an adult. Fortunately for all of us, it's never too late to start being more tolerant.

I cringe when I hear a parent say to a child, "You're being ugly," or "That was stupid," because what a child hears is, "I'm ugly," or "I'm stupid." Just as damaging can be the non-verbal ways of showing intolerance toward children. Examples are a look of disgust, a loud sigh, an eye roll, a sneer, or a turning away from the child. Children need to hear adults distinguish between their behavior and who they are, or they will take those words and actions as a rejection or intolerance of them

It's no different for you as an adult, except instead of others doing it to you, you do it to yourself. You need to become the parent of yourself who makes the distinction between your behaviors and who you are, or else you will continue to struggle with what I am going to address next.

Adults Struggling with Tolerance Do These Things

While it is often easier to observe what you do to others, you need to make it equally important to see and understand your behaviors towards yourself. When you look in the mirror, how do you look at yourself? Do you smile or do you frown? Do you avoid your own eye contact? Some people make the most contemptuous glances at themselves when they look in the mirror. When I was in high school, I heard a speaker say, "If you can't look in the mirror and smile at yourself, something is wrong." This haunted me because I rarely, if ever, smiled at myself. Today, I would encourage him to avoid saying "something is wrong," and replace it with, "you might struggle with self-acceptance."

What else do people do who are intolerant of themselves? I'll hit on a few of the most common ones I see.

Shame and self-loathing. People who can't differentiate between themselves and their behaviors and feelings struggle with shame because they don't see themselves *making* mistakes, they see themselves as *being* mistakes. They get stuck in self-loathing and devaluing their existence because they judge themselves by their behaviors or impulses. It's like people who find out they were the result of an accidental or unwanted pregnancy, and then assume the identity of being someone who is unwanted. Shame leads people to adopt an identity based on their mistakes, failures, or negative beliefs, and not their inherent value.

Perfectionism. This is the vice of those who struggle with being defined by performance. The goal of perfection is to be loved and validated by what you can do. The motto is, "If I can do enough things perfectly enough, then I will be enough," or as I saw boldly printed on my niece's sport uniform a few years ago, "Do more. Be more." Sadly, many people get stuck in a hamster wheel of trying to prove their worth through perfect performance, but because perfection is actually unattainable, they never stop running after it. The bar they set for themselves continues to be just a little too high to reach.

I find the best thing to do with a high bar is walk under it. It might not be as easy as it sounds, but it sure beats chasing the mirage of perfection.

Addictions. Those who have a tolerance deficiency are also prone to addictions when they use substances or behaviors to help them avoid feeling real or perceived pain. Despite the often adverse consequences of addictive behaviors, the need to either cover up or push down pain is so strong that the addicted behavior continues. The more the addiction is leveraged to avoid or cope with the pain the more the addiction is needed. Even further, having the pain keeps getting rewarded by the addictive behavior. For example, as long as one has a lot of pain associated with rejection, he can reward it with drinking alcohol every time he starts to feel it. Any behavior or substance can be addictive as long as it is used to avoid pain.

What a cycle to be stuck in, but there's only one option if you want to get out of it—facing the real or perceived pain and working through it. In other words, you have to increase your tolerance to the pain.

What You are Intolerant of in Others, You are Likely Intolerant of in Yourself

I can guarantee if you are critical toward others you are at least, if not more, critical of yourself. Criticism means you put your personal standards on others and hold them in contempt for not meeting them. When you are critical about something in somebody else, you are reacting to your insecurity about it. You react to what you haven't come to terms with in yourself.

For instance, I might criticize you and call you an entitled little child because you complain too much. Why? Because the last thing I want to be seen as is an entitled complainer, but deep down I know I struggle with it. However, I take the easier route of dealing with it and focus on it in you. This is like one politician focusing on the other politician's unreasonableness while being just as unreasonable. Other common examples of things we project onto others are body image, sexuality, greed, race, education level, intolerance, doubts, laziness, etc. Often in the name of "helping" others with their problems, we are showing what we are most anxious about in ourselves.

If you don't deal with your intolerances, you will project them on others. What I believe is happening on a deeper level is the belief that if you can defeat something in someone else 

(or at least help them do so), then you are reinforcing your belief that it is okay to be intolerant of it in you. Regardless of the intent, the work you must do is on you, or you risk becoming intolerant of others instead of more tolerant of yourself.

What are you intolerant (aka, critical) of in others? In the answer then lies the question: how can you become more tolerant of it in *you*?

Everything in this chapter is about creating more tolerance for anything you've been intolerant of in yourself. Tolerance is truly a radical accepting act, and one you must take seriously because it supports everything you're going to do next.

But first, let's see this in motion...

Chelsea's story

Chelsea, an amazing woman with an extensive background of physical, sexual, and verbal abuse, illustrates the power of learning tolerance for herself. Rising out of her history of poverty and abuse, she became a successful health care professional and advocate for children. As successful as her life had become, she struggled greatly with self-acceptance, carrying a burden of contempt for herself that had been put on her by others throughout her life.

Grace Yourself

Even though she excelled at whatever she did, she still had this nagging sense of incompleteness. She taught me one of the best phrases I've heard in our first session: "Grace Yourself." How foreshadowing this was as the next two years of her treatment was exactly this, giving herself grace, especially in those areas she felt shame.

Chelsea knew she was good, but she had a voice telling her she wasn't. That damning voice was echoed by her ex-husband and family who told her she wasn't enough, while at the same time taking advantage of her generosity. Intellectually, she could see what they were doing, but she was stuck trying to prove to them and herself that she was good, and this kept the door locked to her experiencing the tolerance of herself.

Don't Accept Responsibility for the Irresponsibility or Immaturity of Others

Over time she learned to be more tolerant of the guilt she felt as well as her family's negative perception of her. She gave them back the responsibility for their feelings so that she could take responsibility for hers.

You need to do the same if you are going to move forward in your journey toward acceptance. Without doing this you leave the key to the locked door in the hands of others.

Persistence is Power

Chelsea took to changing her life and taking more responsibility for it like all the other tasks in her life— head on. Like driving with one foot on the gas and one foot on the brake, the journey was jerky, but no matter how difficult it got, she kept going. One week she would be having great breakthroughs and the next week she would hit a block she hadn't anticipated. However, she kept it up and continued to increase her acceptance and tolerance of herself. By staying the course, she changed the course of her life.

As a complete bonus, her family started to change as well. Change in others doesn't always happen when someone changes themselves, but when it does, it's fun to watch. Her family became more open to their own struggles and difficult past, and it opened up new ways for them to be a family. You never know how the changes you make in yourself might impact others to make their own changes.

Tolerance Opens the Door

Chelsea shows what starting with tolerance can do. She unlocked the door, lock by lock, and wrestled it opened. Starting with tolerance, you have the opportunity to do the same. It's going to be hard, but I guarantee you will be better for it.

THE DOOR IS NOW OPEN.

3

Appreciation

Appreciation is finding value in something

My Story with Depression (or How Appreciation Changed My Life)

I always had suspicions my depression was more than bad genes or a lack of antidepressant medication in my body (evidenced by multiple rounds of antidepressants not working), and what I needed instead was a new way to look at my depression problem. The ideas in this chapter were transformational for me because they made all the difference in getting out of the depressive cycles that I found myself in for the first thirty years of my life. Three things happened to bring me to this new way that I needed.

First, in grad school a professor assigned us a workbook where we examined our families through multiple theories. Viewing myself and my family in all the theories, I came out with new explanations of what could be leading to the depressive episodes I was having, which gave me a menu full of ways to solve or treat what I was experiencing.

Second, it was around this time the psychiatrist I was seeing delivered the best intervention for me. After trying four different antidepressants, with the last one numbing the right side of my cheek for several weeks, she looked at me in what would be our final meeting and said, "Mr.

Thompson, I can keep writing you prescriptions, but if nothing in your life changes, you're not going to get better."

I cussed her out in my head. After all, it was her job to fix me, but about two miles down the road from her office, it hit me how right she was. Within six months I made significant changes in my work and relationships. I got curious and saw my depression not as an illness, but as a disorder, as in the way I was living and thinking was dis-ordered. Since I was fortunate not to have the kind of depression requiring medication like some do (and I fully support taking something if it works rather than suffering endlessly), I was able to re-order my life and thoughts in new ways, which greatly reduced my depression. It's like I didn't have a depression *problem*, but rather a depression *solution* that wasn't working for me.

Third, I had a life-altering dream. In the dream my dad was in my front yard talking to me. I pulled out a gun and started shooting him right in the chest. He calmly fell to his knees and kept looking at me in the eyes. Kneeling, seemingly unphased, he said, "You don't have to do it this way." I woke up instantly, eyes wide open, heart pumping. "My God, he's right," I thought, "I don't have to destroy my dad or any other person to change my life." Finally, I realized only I could change my life, and I didn't have to wait on anyone or anything to change. I learned, and am still learning, how to be the active agent in my life rather than a passive participant.

I would lie if I said I've been depression-free after these three experiences. The truth is I still feel down and helpless from time to time, but it is not alarming, threatening, or distressing like it once was. My internal response is, "Mr. Thompson, it's up to you, and unless you make some changes, you're not going to feel better." Then, I get curious and figure out what I can change to get my life back in order. As I sit here reflecting on these experiences, I can appreciate how much value they brought into my life through self-reflection, challenge, and opportunities for change, and how far I've come from being a six-year-old with no hope.

Appreciation is Finding Value in Something

Appreciation is about finding value in something. It's seeing the potential or usefulness of something in a way where you can value what it has to offer. You might not like or even embrace what you see or feel, but you are able to understand that it could make some contribution to your life. For example, have you ever heard or seen a recording of you and then criticized yourself for everything about it, from the way your voice sounded to how big your forehead looked? However, when you got over the initial shock and horror, you used the recording to help you improve—that was appreciation at work.

Have you ever taken up yoga and stuck with it? You may have initially done it because you liked the stretchy pants, strong scents, and trippy music. I bet, though, what kept you doing the awkward stretching, uncomfortable (sometimes painful) poses, and taking instructions from someone with no concept of personal space, was the value you received from it—the connection with your mind and body, the increased balance and flexibility, and the calming effects of the breath and body work.

While tolerance unlocks and opens the door to yourself, appreciation looks for the value of what has always been on the other side. It's like when you were given feedback from a close friend, mentor, or partner, and rather than taking it as criticism, you took it in with appreciation and saw how it could help you. You did this because you valued what they had to say even though it was difficult to hear. This takes you from the initial contemplation in tolerance of "does this have value?" to the interested consideration in appreciation of "what value does it have?"

Appreciation is Not Always Enjoyment

Appreciation is not the enjoyment of someone or something. For instance, I can appreciate you and your influence in my life and not enjoy being around you. I have clients who appreciate the work we do together, but tell me they don't always enjoy the work or me. You can see the value of a failure or mistake in your life, but not like how it feels knowing you made the mistake or the consequences coming from it. You can appreciate the process of getting stronger by working out without enjoying the discomfort and pain it causes your body. Likewise, appreciation is not the mandatory full embrace of something, and it does not require you to put on rose-tinted glasses and try to see the positive in everything. Appreciation is seeing the potential or usefulness of something in a way that you can value what it has to offer.

Appreciation is Fundamentally Curious

Can you find value in what you do and what you bring to your life and to others? If not, can you at least consider the idea that you and your behaviors have value?

You don't have to know your value or the value of what you do before moving forward, you just need to be open to finding it, even if it is hard to see. All of this brings us to curiosity.

Curiosity is your superpower to appreciation and beyond. It is a key to walking through the door to appreciation and to new possibilities for your life. Just as an alchemist is looking to add elements together to make gold, curiosity is the element that, if added to your life, can create real transformation. Let's explore a few things you need to know about curiosity.

Curiosity is the beginning of appreciation. Instead of labeling behaviors as right or wrong, positive or negative, normal or abnormal, and looking for a diagnosis to give yourself, try getting curious instead. When you are curious, behaviors are able to be seen as attempted solutions to life's problems, rather than problems themselves, making them valuable to understand.

Have you ever had the experience of being totally ignored by someone you know in public? You may have felt hurt, ignored, or confused initially, but then you became curious and asked the person about it, only to find out they were in a hurry and didn't even notice you. That's an act of curiosity. By asking your friend, you sought out different possibilities and explanations of what happened, rather than presuming that your interpretation was the only possible explanation.

The more you practice doing this, the better you will get at it, and with what I am going to show you next, you'll be able to open yourself up to a much greater appreciation of yourself.

Curiosity is intentional. Curiosity does not happen by accident, it's something you have to consciously do, and it starts with being open to alternatives. You have to override your human tendency to make snap judgments and react in the moment. Also, it's not a silver bullet for solving all of life's problems, but it is often effective. Let's look in detail at what curiosity does to make appreciation possible.

Curiosity values questions over answers. This means you focus less on finding the right answers to life's problems and instead focus more on asking questions which can open up new worlds and possibilities to you. Let me give you some examples. When confronted with a behavior in your life or attribute about yourself you don't like, try asking: *What else could this mean?* This question keeps us from seeing something from one narrow perspective. For instance, if we do something and the only conclusion we make is that it happened because we were stupid, worthless, or shameful, we risk missing out on alternative ways to see ourselves, such as scared, confused, immature, or feeling unheard. We open up additional possibilities for ourselves with these latter explanations.

You could also try asking yourself: *What emotions or needs might be behind my behavior?* Asking this enables us to address our emotions rather than merely continuing to react to them. Emotions are like the check engine light in your car. The check engine light is the car's way of telling you something is off. The light, like an emotion, is not the problem, just the signal of one. An adverse or unwanted emotion is your internal check engine light, simply conveying to you that something is off and you should check it out and then  make corrections if needed. Getting mad at an emotion is like getting mad at the light in the car—it won't help. Whether you get the message or get messed up by the emotion is up to you.

If these questions aren't helpful you might ask: *How could I address my emotions differently?* Let's say you are avoiding somebody and you don't know why, but you have an emotional response, like anxiousness, around this person. You can try to convince yourself that you should not be anxious, or you could get curious about what your anxiety is trying to tell you. You might realize this person reminds you of somebody else in your life, or that you really want this person's approval, or that you are uncertain if you can trust this person. Whatever the case, you can explore what is behind the emotion so you can make a decision about how you want to interact with them in the future.

Perhaps you could ask: *What are the benefits of this behavior?* You may not know exactly why you are doing something, especially if what you are doing does not seem to be helping your cause. However, in most cases you wouldn't have done it if there wasn't at least some benefit or anticipated benefit. Asking this curious question assumes you are hoping to benefit in some way by what you do, and if this is the case, then you can focus on whether the behavior is worth the benefit.

For example, you might not like that you yell at your kids, but the benefit might be you get their attention and they respond quicker. However, you have to decide if it is worth continuing to yell at them when you know it is not what you want to do. Or, you might find yourself drinking a little too much at social gatherings to have less anxiety and more fun, but at the expense of embarrassment and/or a hangover the next day. Being aware of the benefits helps you understand what you get from the behavior so you can decide if the benefit is worth the consequences.

Another essential question is: *Am I making this worse?* If you are trying to solve a problem and you continue to have the same problem over and over again or it's getting worse, this is the question you need to ask. Then, you can decide if you should continue doing what you are doing or scrap it and try something else. You always want to avoid a situation where you are making a problem worse by how you are trying to solve it.

I remember a time I tried hard to loosen a bolt under my car. I pulled it harder and harder as I got more frustrated that it wouldn't loosen. After exhausting all my energy and coming close to losing my religion, it occurred to me I was turning it the wrong way, and my supposed solution of turning it harder was not helping. I only ceased my self-defeating behavior when I stopped what I was doing, took a pause, and realized this. Once I reversed my motion it released.

It's one thing when it is a car, but what about when it is about a close relationship, or parenting, or managing workplace conflict?

When your solution of giving someone information, sage advice, and opportunities to change isn't working, what do you do? Maybe you give them the same information and advice with more volume and more emotion, hoping they'll finally get it. Or, maybe you threaten them with some consequence until they make the change, but never actually follow through with the threat. If either of these seem like a response you would take then this question is for you. Remember to ask yourself: Am I making this worse by how I am responding? This provides you with a chance to pause and evaluate what you are doing, and then come up with a better solution than something that is clearly not working.

The Power of Curious Questions is the Power to Create New Possibilities

By using questions like these you can open up new possibilities and explanations to help you appreciate who you are and what you have experienced.

Many of us get stuck asking terribly serious and limiting questions like, "What's wrong with me?" or "How do I stop doing this?" when we feel and behave in ways we do not understand or like. These types of questions assume there is no value in the experiences, feelings, or qualities we do have, and severely limit or completely prevent us from getting anything useful out of them.

For example, Ruby, a lady in her 60s, was struggling with motivation, energy, and a depressed mood. Her questions were, "What's wrong with me?" and "Why am I so depressed?" Hearing her talk about going through her mother and stepfather's belongings to get their house ready to sell after they both died, I thought asking a different question might help her best. I said, "I wonder if this could be grief. What could you be grieving right now?" It was then that a light bulb went off for her and she replied, "I think I am finally grieving for my mother [who had died 12 years earlier], but hadn't because my step-father was still alive." New question, new possibility. After this, she allowed herself to grieve and over time her energy returned and her mood lifted.

Curiosity Values Playfulness Over Seriousness

Curiosity requires a playfulness with the situation you are in and the variables involved in it. While you can be playful without being curious, you can't be curious without being at least a little playful. With playfulness a "problem" can be seen instead as an opportunity for learning. Excluding problems needing to be dealt with swiftly or decisively such as cases of imminent danger and/or abuse of others, with most other problems we can be playful and imaginative. Since playfulness is not threatened by ambiguity like seriousness is, you can interact with your problems from different angles and think about all the existing possibilities.

This is like being a kid with a box and a wild imagination. The problem of what to do with the box is quickly solved through playfulness and imagination, because the box is a house and then a car and then a spaceship for stuffed animals and then a treasure chest. A child sees a box and many possibilities for the box limited only by imagination and interest.

Box or Car or Rocket or Robot

When a husband, wife, and his mother came in to consult with me, they brought a problem stuck in seriousness—no one could convince anyone else to behave right. The husband couldn't convince his mother to take care of herself, and the wife couldn't keep the husband from getting upset about his mother, and the mother couldn't convince them she was fine. Then, the husband, referring to something from an earlier session said, "I know I'm not supposed to hold her rope, but she'll just give up if I don't hold it for her." This statement was exactly what was needed to invite curiosity into the situation. By him introducing this metaphor of holding her rope, he opened a new world of playful possibilities.

Whenever you use a metaphor, you can position yourself to be curious because you can explore various meanings which can offer up new solutions.

We were off to the races talking about their rope-holding skills. We talked about how the husband was holding mother's rope, while the wife was holding the husband's rope, but no one was holding the wife's rope. I let them know I was a terrible rope-holder and would be little help. We laughed about the predicament they were in, and I made some crack about the difficulties of having three saviors in one room. From then on, they continued to be playful with their problem and made adjustments to their rope-holding.

Playfulness encounters a problem with the imaginative capacity of a child without having to become childish in the immature sense. We still get to use our adult brains, but with the flexibility of a child's imagination.

Perhaps this is why when Jesus' overly serious disciples asked him questions like "Who's the greatest among us?" he told them, "...unless you change and become like little children, you will never enter the kingdom of heaven." He knew they needed to loosen up and engage life and faith with a more playful imagination like children. This is also why the Zen master Shunryu Suzuki wrote, "In the beginner's mind there are many possibilities, but in the expert's there are few." We need to expand our possibilities at this stage, not limit them, and playfulness does this amazingly well.

Curiosity Values Utility Over Diagnosis

This means shifting away from the way most people view behaviors, which is seeing behaviors as things to be diagnosed, cured, or eliminated, to seeing them as clues for discovering what is going on at a deeper level. Just as a runny nose is a symptom of a cold and not the cold itself, the behavior is a byproduct or symptom of a problem. We learn to utilize behaviors as clues to what the problem is that we need to address. It is about asking, "What is this response showing me about what is really happening on a deeper level?"

Let's say you struggle with constantly questioning your partner, much to your partner's dismay. You can both focus on the over-questioning as the problem, or you can use it to help you identify and work through your deeper struggles with insecurity about the relationship or the fear of losing it. Instead of asking questions for reassurance all the time, you may find a better solution for communicating your love and fear of losing this person without pushing the person away. Once you treat the problem, the symptom is no longer needed.

Procrastination is another behavior we often focus on as the problem rather than as a symptom. Procrastination is a clue that there might be a problem with motivation, fear, or insecurity. It can also be a clue we are not ready to take responsibility for what's on the other side of the activity that we aren't finishing. I had a friend in college who never graduated. Two decades later as my wife and I finally paid off our loans, he is likely still three hours (*three hours!*) short of a degree, and he's a brilliant guy. However, he solved the problem of having to decide what to do after college by never finishing college. Have you ever gotten close enough to reach out and touch the finish line, but didn't?

What would happen if you looked at the areas where you are procrastinating and dealt with your insecurities? Would you finally get married? Have children? Write the book you've always wanted to? Start saving for retirement? Join (and even use) a gym? Learn how to cook? What are you putting off, not because you aren't capable of it, but because of your insecurities or fears?

Utility Over Diagnosis with Children's Behaviors

As a society, we have a tendency to pathologize children's behavior, and I understand why: we need ways to describe what's going on with our children so we can hopefully help them.

What we don't do well is discuss how behaviors or behavioral difficulties are primary ways that children express what is going on in their external and internal environments, such as an overly critical parent, chaos in the family, overwhelming expectations, conflict between parents, poor boundaries in the family, lack of structure and rules, fear, abuse, feeling unsafe, etc.

In the curious frame of behavior as communication, the child's actions, instead of being pathologized, can be valued and understood for what they are highlighting or expressing both about the environment and the child's needs.

Do you remember being a child and getting so upset about something but despite your attempts to call attention to it you were ignored and/or told to stop? Maybe at some point you even stopped trying to call attention to any of your pain or problems, since it didn't seem to matter. However, the subsequent denial, suppression, and avoidance caused its own problems, and if those attempts to keep it down were diagnosed (anxiety, depression, oppositional defiance, etc.), chances are the behaviors got treated rather than utilized to understand you and your needs.

This might leave you with many reactions, such as empathy, outrage, grief, and guilt, and bring up difficult emotions. For those who received mental health or medical treatment as children while having deeper issues ignored or minimized, this can be saddening and even infuriating. Unfortunately, mistakes are made by well-meaning parents and professionals that can have serious consequences. That's not an excuse, but a reality I hope can continue to be challenged and changed.

It's also not to shame or make anyone feel bad who has sought out treatment for their children, as sometimes it is that treatment that was absolutely necessary in improving the quality of a child's life. My plea for all of us is to educate ourselves and take seriously how we interpret and utilize what children are expressing through their behaviors, so we can make the best choices on behalf of them.

In contrast, do you remember a time as a child that someone took the time to listen and understand you? If so, I bet it feels good just thinking about it. My primary care doctor did this when he took time to ask me about what was going on at school when he was treating me for frequent stomach aches in third grade. He picked up on my anxiousness and told me how his daughter had a similar experience when she was my age. His interest and curiosity helped me feel understood and valued, and it made a difference. While you and I needed others to do this for us when we were children, it's now our job as adults to be curious toward ourselves and others (especially children).

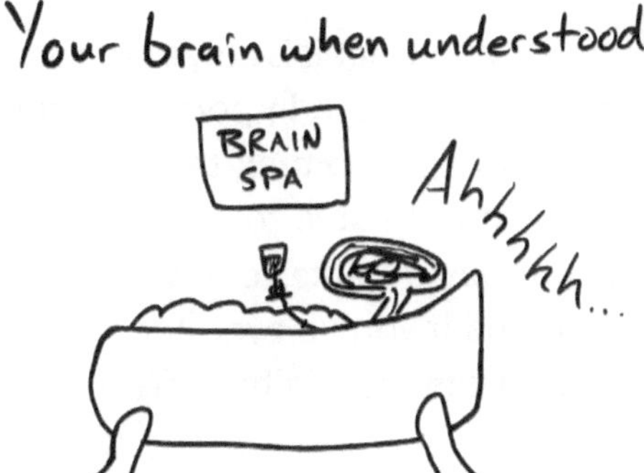

Depression Might Mean You are Overwhelmed

Depression is an example of something often subject to treatment, but not utilization. In the absence of clear biological and medical issues underlying it, depression is often your mind and body's way of expressing a problem of feeling overwhelmed by something like grief, a relationship, a difficult job situation, expectations, responsibilities, or emotions.

By understanding depression as a way to call attention to an overwhelming life situation, you can begin to identify what needs to change in your life. You can start building some momentum by making small changes, and then build on those. One small change could be taking a short walk each day and taking some deep breaths.

I've encountered many depressed people who, by addressing the depressing situation in their life, experienced various levels of relief from their depression. They found a way out of the overwhelm by both dealing with it and working through it. When they let go of some of the weight of the responsibility that wasn't theirs, they were able to feel relief, and this allowed their bodies and minds to stop pushing on the brakes so hard.

Even if the change one feels is only a little diminishment of the depression, it is both important and helpful. It's like a little sliver of light coming through the darkness. While you might not be able to escape the clutches of depression, you may be able to loosen its grip on you ever so slightly, and if you've ever been depressed, you know a little relief can make a big difference.

Depression Might Mean You Need "Deep Rest"

Jeff Foster, a contemporary spiritual teacher, offers another creative way to look at depression. One day when he heard the word "depressed," he noticed how it sounded like "deep rest." Maybe the struggle you are in, he concluded, means you need deep rest from trying to be who you think you need to be for yourself and everyone else. I agree, it's exhausting!

With the explanation of depression as needing deep rest from trying too hard to be what you think you need to be for yourself and others, you can accept the responsibility for taking a break from the character you are playing, get some rest, and then learn how to live in a way that doesn't deplete all your energy.

At the same time, this does not mean it won't take energy and effort to change, something depression makes you feel like you don't have. Understanding the cause of your depression gives you the capacity and responsibility to do something different, to take action. It often feels easier to take the route of inaction (sleeping and not moving) and numbing (drugs, alcohol, TV) because it is easier at first...until it's not, and you find yourself in more difficult situations, like potentially losing relationships, jobs, or your health.

Ben's Diagnosis of Stuckness Manual (B-DSM)

The Bible for mental health and medical professionals is the *DSM*, which stands for the *Diagnostic and Statistical Manual of Mental Disorders*. If you have ever received a mental health diagnosis, it came from this book.

I decided to bring some curiosity to this decidedly uncurious work, which left me with my own version of the *DSM*, which I call Ben's Diagnosis of Stuckness Manual. I thought about calling it the BDSM, but that acronym was already taken. In my pretend manual I take commonly known disorders and problems and identify where someone is stuck. This is in no way meant to replace any serious diagnosis of a mental disorder, only to be curious and creative with it. However, it can be easy to get stuck with a diagnosis rather than find a way out. My pretend manual seeks to take a diagnosis or psychological term and put it in terms of how one might be stuck, which could then allow someone to get curious about how to get unstuck. Here's a look into the manual:

- *Anxiety:* stuck seeing only negative outcomes in the future regardless of what I do
- *Depression:* stuck seeing myself only helpless and/or hopeless in present and future situations
- *Generalized Anxiety:* stuck worrying about everything, especially at 2 AM
- *Obsessive-Compulsive Disorder (OCD):* stuck doing things I think I have to do in order to keep bad things from happening
- *Seasonal Affective Disorder:* stuck in a season of the year I don't like while longing for a better one
- *Phobia:* stuck in fear of something
- *Marital discord:* stuck doing marriage in a way I don't like or with a partner I can't get along with
- *Narcissism:* stuck trying to cover up a deep insecurity about myself by trying to get others to accept a false, grandiose persona I've created
- *Grief:* stuck on the loss of something or someone
- *Adjustment disorder:* stuck trying to keep things the way they were before a difficult event or transition happened
- *Attention Deficit Disorder (ADD):* stuck in perpetual distraction
- *Attention Deficit Hyperactivity Disorder (ADHD):* stuck in perpetual distraction, turbo mode
- *Addiction:* stuck avoiding real or perceived pain by using short-term solutions like abusing drugs and alcohol, gambling, or excessive social media scrolling
- *Post-Traumatic Stress Disorder (PTSD):* stuck reliving experiences and feelings of an event after

it happened

- *Codependency:* stuck taking responsibility for other people and believing that's what they need from you (and then stuck with all the anxiety and stress coming from this arrangement)

With these descriptions, one could effectively design a treatment to get unstuck. This is what I tend to think about when I am with people—how are they stuck and how do they get unstuck? What log in the stopped up river needs to be kicked so the river can flow again? If someone can see where they are stuck, then the good news is that they can find a way to get unstuck.

Curiosity Cured My Daughter's Phobia

Since curiosity is so elemental in creating space for appreciation to happen, I want you to see it at work in the following story. It took intentionally interacting with what was in front of us so we could find a solution.

One day my daughter suddenly developed a phobia of "Mama hairs," and would stop in her tracks when she saw a Mama hair on the floor and wouldn't move or cross it. We would have understood this if my wife was Medusa, but my wife has long, beautiful dark hair, resulting in the occasional stray strand on the floor. All of our logical, reasonable, and rational statements like "Don't be silly, it's only a hair," and "You know it can't hurt you," failed like anything rational does with a two-year-old. We couldn't convince her to simply step over the hair, and when the question, "Oh no, do we need to seek out a therapist for this?" formed in our minds, we decided to get curious: what else could this mean? How could we find a way to play around with this phobia and change her phobic response?

First, we decided one significant problem she had was us: two overly serious and anxious parents needing to lighten up. And what's lighter and less serious than a single strand of hair? We decided instead of the context where she is a victim of Mama hairs, she needed a context where she could be a hero and save her overly serious parents from the hair and their seriousness. With a new plan in place, I waited for her to leave the room, and when she did, I laid down, put a Mama hair on my chest, and acted like I was being held captive by it, stuck under its weight and power. We yelled out to our daughter to come save me from the villainous hair. She responded by looking at me like I was crazy and proceeded to remove the hair, becoming a hero instead of a victim, and helping her uptight parents loosen up. Her phobia vanished shortly after this.

When we gave her an opportunity to recast her relationship to her fear, she was able to respond out of her new found power to solve her problem. Likewise, when we were able to view her phobia in a non-pathological and more meaningful light, we were able to respond to it more creatively. All behavior is meaningful, we just have to figure out how to utilize it.

In your life, are you interacting with your problems in ways that are keeping you from solving them? How can you view your struggles in new ways that bring about new possible solutions?

Appreciation is about taking what is in front of you and finding the value in it. When you create a context through curiosity to appreciate something, you can solve "serious" problems. This powerful idea launched an entire industry that you've probably partaken in: personality tests.

The Power of Personality Tests (It has Little to do with the Tests Themselves)

How many different personality tests have you taken in your life? I'm up to seven or eight. Usually it's part of therapy or a job training or at the behest of an overeager friend who just took one and it *completely* changed their life.

The tests are created by compiling a group of tendencies or characteristics and then representing those groups with a number, a four-letter code, an animal, or labeling it a voice or a gift, and voila, you have a personality test. This has led to a massively lucrative industry around personality tests— books, online courses, advanced trainings, super-advanced trainings, weekend retreats, retreat centers (borderline communes in some cases), and so on.

I tell you this because I want you in on a little joke: personality tests are essentially about appreciation, and that's it. The tests create a context where you can get curious about behaviors and tendencies, which allows you then to ultimately appreciate them. You learn that your idiosyncratic behaviors are there for a reason, and as such, you can appreciate them rather than resist them in yourself and others. This is the power of giving something meaning through curiosity. I also think you could skip the tests, do what I am talking about in this book, and find yourself in a similar place, because you are learning to value you and find meaning in all you do. If you need a test to do this, go for it, because in the end if you become more appreciative of you and others, it's a win.

The Main Obstacle to Appreciation is Lack of Curiosity

Since curiosity is a powerful tool, the lack of it is one of the main obstacles to appreciation. If you are unable to see something in alternative ways, you won't be able to find value or meaning in it, and you'll remain in an inflexible position toward yourself and your behaviors.

Curiosity helps more cats than it kills, although I have no stats to back this up, just a bunch of surviving cats. Curiosity is how a cat figures out the world and how to survive. Inevitably this does lead to the proverbial cat stuck in the top of the tree or in a bag However, all this curiosity comes in handy when they need to survive. It's their way of figuring out the world and how to navigate it.

Fortunately, you are human and don't have to get stuck in things or constantly rub up against your surroundings to see if they are stable (such behavior in the latter case could get you arrested). As a human you can get curious simply by asking good questions, reading a book, finding out how other people solve their problems, trying on new explanations and meanings, seeking out a coach or therapist, and so on.

Cats get stuck in bags, humans get stuck in diagnoses, certainty, and ways of thinking. I am not suggesting shirking all diagnoses, throwing caution to the wind, and ending your antidepressant and anti-anxiety medications. What I am advocating is in order to avoid being stuck in a diagnosis, get curious and do something different in your life. A diagnosis is what a healthcare professional needs so they can prescribe the best treatment they know. However, sometimes it's not just the medication or treatment that isn't working, but it's the way you're doing life. Take your meds, but continue working on your life. Curiosity puts you in a new frame where you can appreciate yourself and the things you do so you can utilize them rather than try to avoid them.

Appreciation Avoids Elimination

In third grade art class we drew self-portraits. I showed mine to the art teacher and she told me it was missing something. "What did I miss?" I asked. "Your cowlick. It's one of your features." For those not familiar with cowlicks, imagine what your hair would look like if a cow licked straight up the back of your head. The hair sticking straight up to the sky waving to all those around you, that is your cowlick.

"I can't draw that," I thought. I mean, this feature was the bane of my mother's existence every time she did my hair for church and family pictures. She couldn't get it to stay down no matter what she did. Now, my art teacher was telling me to embrace this absolute nuisance in my life. Not wanting to disappoint my art teacher, I drew it, and it might sound dramatic, but it changed my relationship to my cowlick forever. It was now a valued part of me. To this day I smile when it proudly pops up. I don't remember my art teacher's name, but I remember the amazing lesson she taught me. It wasn't the elimination of the cowlick I needed, it was the appreciation of it.

Now You Can See What's Behind the Door

What are you tempted to keep away from yourself and on the other side of the acceptance door? As you find the value in yourself and the meaningfulness of your behaviors, you are moving through to the other side of the door. You are no longer resisting what's on the other side. All the work in toleration and appreciation prepares you for the next part of your journey: reconciliation.

4

Reconciliation

Reconciliation is the rejoining and reconnecting of ourselves to ourselves

Reconciliation of Ourselves to Ourselves

Reconciliation is the rejoining and reconnecting of ourselves to ourselves in order to become more whole.

While tolerance and appreciation opens up the door to ourselves, reconciliation is learning to embrace what's on the other side. We receive back into ourselves any parts of us that we've alienated, feared, or denied by choosing to take an active role in accepting them.

You Possess Your Parts or Become Possessed by Them

Whenever you have thoughts like, "Part of me wants to do one thing, while another part of me wants to do something else," you are simply experiencing different parts of yourself. When I talk about parts from here on out, this is what I mean.

You tend to have parts you are comfortable with because you believe you "should" have them, and parts you struggle with because you believe you "shouldn't" have them. The "should have" parts are usually the nice, polite, loving, caring, empathic, happy parts, while the "shouldn't have" parts are usually things like anger, hatred, selfishness, fear, anxiety, and sadness. You learned what parts you should and should not have largely based on what your caregivers and the culture around you shamed or valued, accepted or rejected.

EMOTIONS	
Okay	Not okay
Happiness	Anger
Love	Hate
Gratitude	Sadness
Peacefulness	Anxious
Excitement	Fearful

Reconciliation then is the process of identifying parts, valuing them, and bringing them back into yourself so that you can take greater responsibility for them. Because they are part of you again, you can now direct them rather than be directed by them. For instance, if you can be reconciled with the parts of you that are angry, you can learn to value them for the message they bring you and direct their energy in resourceful ways, rather than react to them in ways that hurt you and others. It is far better to learn how to utilize anger than it is to manage it or be driven around by it, and you can't utilize it until you reconcile with it.

To repress, suppress, learn to cope with, or try to eliminate certain parts of you tends to set you up for more problems because if you avoid them like this they will continue to show up in ways where you have little control—rage, overwhelming sadness, dissociation, high (or low) sexual urges, compulsive eating or exercising, etc. The goal is to learn how to possess your parts rather than to be possessed by them. They can own you, or you can own them, but try as you might, you cannot simply get rid of them.

A Quick Glance at Reconciliation

Reconciliation is not an exoneration of all wrongdoing or mistakes because "that's just who I am (or was)." Rather, it's taking greater responsibility for yourself by accepting your ability to produce all sorts of behaviors, thoughts, emotions or inclinations. Reconciliation brings you closer to your alienated, ignored, and denied parts so that you can choose what to do with them, rather than being controlled by them.

Reconciliation is also not a one-time event, it's a continual process. It would be nice if you could have one moment of total reconciliation and then never have to revisit it again, but it doesn't ever happen this way. You will be faced with new parts of yourself as you grow, and you will also experience old parts in new ways. Even those who have profound spiritual experiences through sacred rituals, weekend retreats, near-death experiences, or psychedelic trips, must still make the continued choice of how they will be reconciled to themselves. No matter how great the trip, one still has to come home.

Finally, reconciliation is not a passive process. It's an intentional and conscious engagement in the rejoining of yourself and your separated parts. While reconciliation is often difficult at first, it becomes easier with practice. Your responsibility right now is to show up and do the work to make reconciliation possible, and you can start by taking some of the following postures in your life.

Postures of Reconciliation

Your posture determines the position you are taking toward something, and in this work, you need to posture yourself in ways to help you succeed. Take these postures and you will be set up for a much smoother experience in your journey towards reconciliation.

Becoming Receptive

A receptive posture is one in which you are curious and open. If you are applying the first two levels (tolerance and appreciation) then you're already doing this. You're welcoming whatever comes

your way as something with value, and this is precisely where reconciliation begins.

Have you ever said or done something to others, like lie or yell or try to manipulate them in some way, even though you knew it wasn't right? Part of you knew not to do it, but you didn't act out of that part, you acted (or reacted) out of another part of you that felt threatened or insecure. Because of your actions, you had a choice to make—you could either cover up what you did through denial or defensiveness ("it's not my fault, you or something else *made* me do this"), or you could be accountable to your behavior and reconcile with it and the person you treated badly.

Only with a receptive posture can you be reconciled with any part of yourself. This posture positions you to welcome your part, own it, and ultimately bring it back into you where you can be compassionate towards it and learn to engage it responsibly. Once you own it, then you can be truly accountable to others and ultimately become fully responsible for your behavior.

Becoming Non-Reactive

The non-reactive posture is defined by being able to respond to something out of thoughtful consideration rather than emotions. It does not mean you don't have any emotions or anxiety. Rather, the goal is to be connected with yourself enough so that you can avoid reacting out of unchecked or undirected emotions or anxiety.

For example, it's annual review day and your boss calls you in to go over your performance on the latest HR review form. She goes over her evaluation of you and points out some areas you need to improve because you are only "meeting expectations," rather than "exceeding expectations." Before you know it you start to feel the tension rising in your body and your face begins to flush. The thoughts begin to flood in about how inaccurate she is because she doesn't even observe you working, so how can she rate you, and even more so, how you can even meet expectations when you are doing the work of three people... and the reactions never stop.

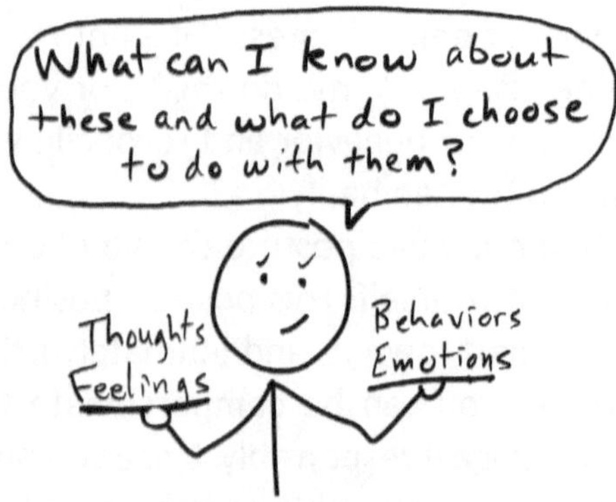

Taking a non-reactive posture might look something like this: you finish out the formalities of the situation without screaming, take a copy of the review, and find a place to go to let the adrenaline wear off. You do what you need to do to feel calm, and instead of typing up your resignation letter, you take your time going over the review with as much objectivity as you can. You stay present and aware, consider what is in front of you and then take time to decide what you want to do next.

Reactivity keeps you from reconciling parts to yourself because you are connected to the anxiety produced by those parts rather than being connected to the parts themselves. Being non-reactive allows you to interact, acknowledge, and eventually even to accept the parts you are anxious about, allowing you then to choose how you want to respond to it.

Becoming the Guide

The receptive and non-reactive postures make the guiding posture possible. In a guiding posture, you are not being forceful or like a dictator with your parts, but instead you are able to guide them in a direction that you believe is best for you.

Can you think of something you do now that used to cripple you? Let's take dancing as an example. Think of your first dance. How did you feel—scared, reluctant, fearful of messing up or looking foolish? Now, though, you might have no problem getting on the dance floor and busting out a few moves, even to your family's embarrassment (in my case). How did you move from fearful to confident? For me, I had to become more receptive to the idea of dancing and less anxious and reactive about what I might look like while dancing. Whatever feelings I might have had before were held in check as I learned how to dance better and/or learned how to not care as much about how I looked while dancing. This made it possible for me to get out on the dance floor.

You will find that you are ready to guide yourself once you're receptive and non-reactive to what is going on inside you. The guiding posture is the final act of reconciliation because you are able to both possess your parts and direct them at the same time, even if (or perhaps especially if) it feels awkward.

This dance with yourself is exactly what a good ballroom dancing couple does. One leads while the other follows. Both roles are necessary for the dance, but if the partners are confused or competitive in their roles, the dance won't go well. The leader can't allow

the follower to lead, and the follower can't take control of the leader. When the roles are clear and respected, the leader doesn't lead with force, but by guiding their steps.

By becoming the leader of you and your parts, you are determining the dance and the direction of your life. If you are not being driven by your emotional parts, you can lead yourself toward the places you want to go, and then you can continue to advance on your acceptance journey.

Accepting Limits as the Key to More Power in Your Life

One important thing to keep in mind is that even as you develop the power of these postures that you still have limits. Accepting the reality that you have certain limits is your key to greater power in your life. In a world of self-help literature telling you how "unlimited" you are and how, "You can do anything you put your mind to," this idea might seem counterintuitive.

When you accept certain limits, you quit trying to function beyond your power. This allows you to put greater focus and emphasis on your true power–the ability to make decisions and take actions consistent with what you want most.

Influence, energy, and time

The three limits you need to accept in order to grow in your power are:

- *Influence*: how much persuasion or power I have over myself or other people's perceptions of me
- *Energy*: how I invest my resources and where I apply effort in my life
- *Time*: how I prioritize what I do in my life

The Most Important Person You Can Influence is You

Perception management can be a full-time job. You can't be all things for all people no matter how hard you try, and in attempting to do so, you'll continue to give up more and more of yourself. Think about social media influencers who, in order to stay relevant or interesting, eventually become absolutely driven by their audience by their comments, likes/dislikes, number of views, or outside sponsors incentivizing them to use their products (or lack thereof). The "influencers" ultimately become tools of influence.

Influencer Double Take

Accepting the limits of your influence means you don't have to be driven by what you think others need or want you to be. True power in life is about knowing who you are, what you believe, and then living those things out. If I change myself to get you to like me or buy from me, I am manipulating you and am being manipulated myself. It's like being a salesperson for a product you don't really like, but pretending you do so you can sell it. Have you ever found yourself in this predicament?

When you know who you are and what you stand for, you can then be truly influential. Reconciliation requires you to be true to yourself and your beliefs, and not trying to influence others by being someone you're not. You must become responsible for influencing yourself through the pursuit of truth.

You Decide Where You Will Put Your Energy

You can learn good sleeping, eating, and exercising habits to increase your energy, but you still have limits, requiring you to make choices about where to put your energy. You can even manipulate this to some extent with drugs from caffeine to cocaine, but those come at the expense of an eventual crash. Greg McKeown wrote a brilliant book called *Essentialism* in which he argues that instead of investing your energy in many different directions, it would be far better to put more energy in fewer, but more essential areas.

When you decide where you will put your energy, you have more control over it than it has control over you. This sounds obvious, but how often do you find yourself overextending yourself and feeling stressed out because you have more to-dos than todays? Instead of trying to figure out how to do more, you might be better off figuring out where you want to put your energy. Far from limiting you, focusing your energy makes you more powerful in the areas of your focus, just like a laser is more powerful because it is focused light. You gain more power when you take the responsibility for where your energy is going, but to do this you must challenge yourself to first define and then pursue what is most important to you.

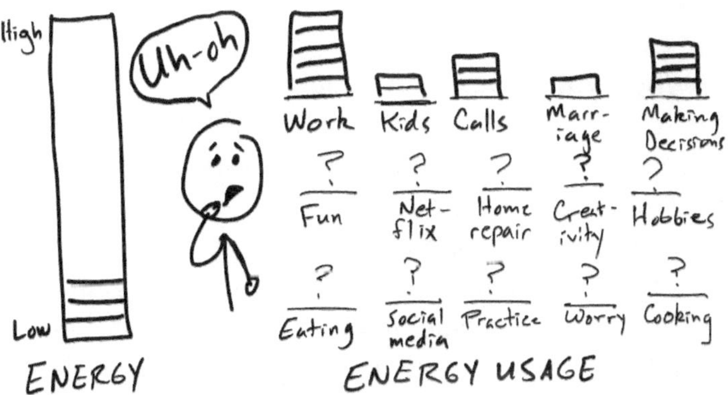

In terms of reconciliation, you must ask yourself if you will spend your energy and resources avoiding the parts of yourself that you are uncomfortable with, or if you will spend it on how you can be reconciled with them? Avoidance and reconciliation both take energy, but only reconciliation will lead to a resolution. And resolution is not only a conservation of energy, but can even be a profound source of it. It's like finally completing a project important to you and then feeling a release to pursue something new.

Time Can't Be Made, Only Spent

You are going to die at some point (although science and its tech icon patrons are feverishly trying to change this) and your time will run out. People don't always like to be confronted with this. The point is, like limited energy, you have limited time, and you need to accept this and become more 

intentional with how you use it. You can't make time; you can only spend it.

When you choose how you spend your time, you get to invest it in accordance with your values. Your intentional time investment is a form of power, and the truth is that either you will choose what to do with your time or someone or something else will. Valuing your time is valuing you, and how you spend your time reflects how you value yourself. So when you look at your time bank account charges and pending items, what does it reveal?

Reconciliation of yourself to yourself happens when you know more about who you are as well as who you are not, and how the choices you make with your influence, energy, and time help you to further define who you are. However, you can't be fully reconciled to yourself if you are blocking or resisting any parts of yourself or your story, and that's where our attention needs to turn now.

Without Reconciliation, We are Subject to Reactivity

Reactivity is a response to something either internal or external with one question: What do I do with this? When we don't know what to do with certain parts of ourselves or feel threatened by them, we tend to react to them in extremes by either over-*expressing* them or over-*suppressing* them. These over-reactions can cause serious problems for ourselves.

The following are just a few examples of ways that we might over-*express* some of these areas of our lives.

Sexuality. This happens when we primarily connect with others through sex to the diminishment of other areas, having sexual encounters that are unsafe or that one is not ready for, or identifying primarily by sexual preference.

Sadness. This occurs when you see everything as negative and bad, feel completely helpless about feeling better, or base your identity on your hurt, pain, or suffering.

Doubt. Attacking everyone else's beliefs, doubling down on a position despite clear evidence to the contrary, trying to change other people's minds when they are not asking you to, or completely giving up on believing in anything, are ways that doubt is often over-expressed.

Perhaps we swing to the other extreme and move towards over-*suppression* of these parts of ourselves which might look something like this:

Sexuality. If you notice you are refusing to learn about your sexuality, shaming yourself or others for feeling sexual, avoiding relationships, or calling yourself or others perverts for their sexual interests, you are likely over-suppressing sexuality.

Sadness. This occurs when you push sadness deep down inside to avoid dealing with it, cover it up by pretending to be happy and unaffected by it, or by telling everyone you are okay when you are not. When sadness is suppressed it is often expressed through depression and physical ailments.

Doubt. Avoiding any evidence suggesting your belief is not accurate or correct, doubling down on your positions, shaming others for their doubts, and pretending you agree with everyone around you are often signs of an over-suppression.

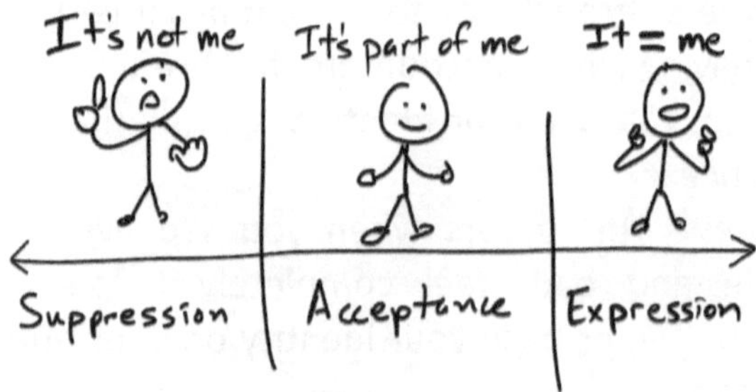

When you reduce your reactivity, you avoid the extremes of over-expression or over-suppression, and can find a healthy place in the middle where you can experience them with both acceptance and openness.

Reconciling with Hate

Hate is one of those emotions or feelings most of us are conflicted about and struggle to know how to accept in our lives. It's a shadow we try to avoid rather than to bring it into the light. Some of us grew up hearing our parents telling us to not even use the word "hate." While I haven't found much good in living in a hateful state or being hateful, I have found it useful to pay attention to it and not just to exile it.

I believe our culture has become so uncomfortable with hate that we've become almost entirely reactive to it. We seem to express it in harmful ways, deny that it's there, or focus entirely on locating it in others. Hurting others through it or hiding it from ourselves has only seemed to increase its power and create greater division. Exclusively focusing on the hate others have has kept us from addressing it within ourselves. Only in owning the hate that we feel can we then begin to understand it and take responsibility for it. Until this happens, we will continue to merely react to it and put it onto others, rather than deal with it and take responsibility for it. If we don't change our relationship to hate, we will only keep hurting ourselves and others.

Once we're able to become increasingly receptive and non-anxious towards hate, we can then recognize hate as a signal of a strong emotion toward something. Understanding that this is a signal, we can then make intentional decisions for the greatest good. For instance, hating bad treatment of others can be helpful in deciding how to put a stop to it. Hating the way we feel when we are at work might be an indication we need to find a new job. When guided, hate can help us get important things done. Hating war and violence can lead to finding better ways to love and treat others. Realizing we hate or are intolerant of someone simply because they are different from us in some way like race, religion, nationality, sports team affiliation, socio-economic class, or political party, can help lead us to deal with our prejudices and commit to some serious work on ourselves.

Three Internal Formidable Foes to Reconciliation at this Stage

When you open the door to yourself, you choose to face what you were once avoiding. This is why reconciliation is not easy, and it is why most of us have not done it. Lack of education about this reconciliation, fear of what you don't understand, and confusion about it, are all reasons for this, but these are all external challenges. Here I want to address the obstacles that are *inside* of us when it comes to doing this work. To address your internal foes is to increase your capacity to respond both internally and externally.

Comparison rejects who you are. Comparison sets you up in your mind against examples you think you have to be like before you can be reconciled to yourself. As a result, you keep at a distance any parts of yourself not fitting the mold of who you think you should be. You can't be reconciled to yourself if you believe that to be good you have to be someone else.

Here's a great way to discover if this is impacting you. Fill in the blank: *Until I am like _______________, I'm not good enough.* It might be a sibling, parent, co-worker, pastor, podcaster (or latest guest on a podcast), social media influencer, or some giant in your career field. Who comes to mind?

With the blank filled in, think about all the ways you would have to change to become like them. You might have to look differently, talk differently, have the same degree as them, have the same amount of followers, have compliant children like they do, and so on. What do they have that you feel like you have to have? What parts of you would you have to change or get rid of in order to be them?

None of this is to say there is anything wrong with wanting to exhibit and possess some of their qualities. Modeling after somebody can be a great way to create change in your life, but if you do it in order to achieve self-acceptance, then it is really an ongoing act of rejection toward yourself. You end up merely idolizing or imitating someone rather than modeling yourself after them, and you simply cannot accept yourself if you are trying to be somebody else. That road ends with an

unfulfilling lament of "that's it," because while working towards becoming them you didn't become yourself, and that's ultimately what you needed (even if it wasn't what you thought you wanted). Here are a few of the models/comparisons/idols I have:

Hal: best-selling author, coach, engaging speaker

>*Milton:* psychiatrist, therapist, highly perceptive, heavily influenced the fields of therapy and coaching
>*Mark:* brother, freak athlete, brilliant mind, my most constant comparison since a small child
>*Tony:* engaging speaker, master of influence, high energy, huge following, ultra-wealthy
>*Shawn:* gifted therapist, influencial, extrovert, infectious personality, strongly convicted in his faith

When I live in comparison to these guys, I feel like I am not smart, athletic, spiritual, energetic, wealthy, or influential enough. This leads me to wondering if I can ever be "enough" because I will never measure up to them (especially collectively!). While it was Theodore Roosevelt who said, "Comparison is the thief of joy," I would add that it is also a thief of reconciliation because comparison keeps you in a place of rejecting yourself.

Knowing your model/comparison/idol list can reveal a lot to you. Fortunately, not one of the people on my list would tell me I have to be like them to be successful. They would, compassionately and directly, admonish me for this belief, and insist that success is becoming the best Ben Thompson I can be. This idea of having to be a clone of a successful person has to be put to bed. Until we believe we are good enough the way we are, we cannot become a more reconciled version of ourselves.

Certainty inhibits progress. If you believe you have to understand everything about a part of you or have the part completely mastered before you are reconciled to it, you're going to struggle with reconciliation. If this is your assumption then you won't move forward until you are certain you have this part all figured out and under control. It's like waiting to commit to a relationship before you are certain the other person is perfect for you and will never hurt you, or waiting to have children until you know you will be a perfect parent. When certainty is the goal, you create specific and unattainable conditions that have to be met before you can act, and therefore you do nothing.

Even if you do somehow miraculously manage to meet those conditions, you then become subject to those conditions being maintained, and you end up spending your time and energy trying to keep them met. Have you ever had the experience of finally getting something you were certain would make you feel awesome about yourself, and it did, until it didn't anymore? You went on a date with that special person, or finally landed that dream job, or finally bought that car, and while it was great at first, it became harder and harder to keep the feeling it gave you. Then, you get depressed or feel defeated when you get let down or disappointed by it. This is what happens when you make reconciliation conditional on certainty—it only lasts as long as the conditions can be sustained.

The only condition necessary for reconciliation to begin is a willingness to accept back into yourself whatever you have avoided or kept out.

Denial blocks access. Denial comes in two types. The first type of denial is pretending something didn't happen or doesn't exist, like a drinking problem, a lie we told, or an event in our life. The denial is all about self-protection and the avoidance of something that you are unwilling to face.

The second type of denial is a refusal to admit how something from your past affected you or someone else. An example of this would be a man I knew who was abused as a child, but played it off by saying it was "no big deal" or "it wasn't that bad." He maintained his denial for the next thirty years by overcompensating for it through acts of proving his strength and power. Sadly, this took the form of treating others in a similar way he had been treated. He adopted the behavior of his abuser to prove his strength over the abuse. Like him, if you work to stay in denial of the impacts of something in your life, continuing to try to prove that it did not affect you, then you might find that you act in ways that harm yourself and others all because of your denial.

Realizing you've harmed others through your denial and overcompensation can create an extremely heavy experience inside of you. It's like a divine slap in the face. If this ever occurs to you, reach out and get help as you work through it. You don't have to eliminate or exile yourself, but you do have to open yourself up to it.

Either type of denial blocks reconciliation because denial is a rejection of an internal or external experience in your life. It's like a child closing his eyes in the middle of a room and believing others can't see him or what he did because he can't see it. How ridiculous...when someone else does it. Just know that no matter how long or how tight you close your eyes to something, it's not going to go away. Instead, you become so insulated or isolated from it that your protection becomes your prison *and* your defense. Only in facing something can you accept it, reconcile it, and become more complete.

Coming Out of Denial is the Beginning of the Healing Process

A common revelation I hear in my work with people is about abuse. Something happened and they have either repressed or avoided talking about for years, for reasons such as protecting the abuser, being seen as weak (especially for men), fear of retaliation, guilt and shame they somehow brought it on themselves, fear of not being believed, or fear of what will happen emotionally to them if they talk about it.

Until a person is able to finally confide in someone safe and come out of the denial that the abuse happened, the healing process can't start. This is an act of reconciliation itself—something happened and it matters that it happened. The receptive posture toward the abuse experience allows the person to understand the effects it had on their life and behavior. *Read this carefully:* It's not acceptance of the abuse itself or the abuser that's important, it's acceptance that it happened and it affected you.

Reconciliation Happens When You Take the Past into Account, Not When You Get Past the Past

The way to experience more wholeness is through reconciliation, and it is not always an easy task with some of your parts and life experiences. I want you to notice how nowhere in this chapter have I told you that you have to be okay with anything in your life or to overlook its effects on you. I personally know how offensive it feels to be told to find the silver-lining in something or to just "get over it." I've also been a recipient of the go-to-hell stare when I've said some version of "get over it" to someone I was trying to help. You do not have to like something or dismiss the harm of something in order to experience reconciliation, in fact you *can't* do that and move forward, you must instead take it into account.

Say for example that you decided to reconcile with someone who hurt you, you didn't do so by dismissing what they did or pretending that what they did had no negative effects on you. Moving towards reconciliation means that you chose to continue in a relationship with a full accounting of the hurtful experience or past action. You reconciled because the other person acknowledged the hurt and took some responsibility for it. Then, together you took responsibility for how you were going to move forward in the relationship. To reconcile with yourself you must acknowledge your past, choose to pursue a relationship with yourself despite any past transgressions, and take responsibility for the relationship you are going to have with yourself going forward. This responsibility includes catching yourself when you try to use your past against yourself, even though you've reconciled with it. You don't have to get past your past, you have to move forward with your past taken into account.

Learn to Own What You Disown, or What You Disown Will Own You

Have you ever been intrigued by seeing a really sweet woman married to an abrasive, stubborn man, or a nice, soft-spoken man married to a bossy, critical woman? Have you ever wondered how someone who is tightly wound up ends up marrying a loose, spontaneous partner with seemingly no cares in the world? Have you ever been strangely attracted to someone else and not known why? I believe this is due to what I call *projective attraction*, which means what you are attracted to in others is what you want to be more like—that you want what they have.

If you are or have been in a close relationship with someone, chances are you were attracted to your partner because they exhibited something you admired. Your unconscious hope was that their admirable qualities would rub off on you. However, as it usually goes, instead of them rubbing off on you, they eventually rubbed you the wrong way. In a twist of irony, you might end up resenting your partner for possessing something that you once admired and you discover that they've yet to be successful in giving it to you.

One of my biggest initial attractions to my wife was her conviction and decisiveness. She knew what she wanted to do and did it, and didn't do what she didn't want to do. One time we were at a pre-screening of a movie looking for a place to sit. We started to sit somewhere and a lady piped up in a snooty voice, "These seats are for press members only." My wife, without missing a beat, looked at her squarely in the eye and stated confidently, "We *are* the press," and we sat down. Wow! What conviction, and on something only partially true in the moment. I was so attracted to this conviction and decisiveness in that moment because I wanted to be more like her, rather than the overly jellyfish-like "nice guy" I often defaulted to in my life.

Over time her conviction and decisiveness started to tick me off, especially when she used it with me. She would get an idea in her head of something she wanted and would not budge. Her decisiveness and conviction made me uncomfortable, but what I really wanted was to find my own conviction. The reason I became such a nice, conflict-avoidant man, despite how much it cost me, was to avoid having to make decisions or taking a stand that might create conflict with someone. It was my way of protecting my fragile ego. Instead of using my wife to wear the conviction pants for me, I needed to own in myself what I disowned about me.

Another reason to learn how to own what you've disowned is this: it helps you avoid the dark side of projective attraction, which is finding someone who is at an unhealthy extreme of what you want to be and using them to be that thing for you. Owning yourself keeps you from situations like finding a rebel to be rebellious for you, or marrying a jerk because you need someone to speak up for you, or getting into a relationship with someone with divergent views from your family because you are afraid to communicate your changing beliefs to them. In all these situations you give up your ownership and responsibility, and you miss the chance to do the work for yourself. When you do the work for yourself, you grow.

Once you take on the responsibility for what you've disowned, you can commit to doing the work of creating it in your life. I once heard Tony Robbins say to someone, "If you don't own what you disowned, what you disowned will end up owning you." Until you take ownership of what you've disowned, you will live in the outward pursuit of something you want internally.

It's Not About What You've Done, It's About Coming Back Home

The story of the Prodigal Son in the Bible illustrates this idea of reconciliation. A son asks to receive his inheritance from his father while his father is still alive, and his father gives it to him. Instead of being wise with his new found wealth, he leaves home, gallivants about doing extravagant things, and ends up throwing it all away.

Out of funds, friends, and food, he decides to come home. We expect his father to chastise him and deny him a place back home, or at least make him earn his way back, but in a dramatic twist, the father runs out to meet him, throws his arms around him in a loving embrace, and brings him home for a homecoming feast.

The story then pans over to the son's older brother. This brother is not thrilled about what's happening. He watches his brother come home after squandering the family wealth while he stayed home and respected his father. Nothing in his mind warrants the over-the-top homecoming celebration from his dad. In his mind this is an act of total foolishness. We might call it enabling today. However, the celebration is not

about what his brother did, the celebration is about the brother's coming back home.

Coming back to yourself regardless of where you've been and what you've done is always worth celebrating. It's throwing yourself a homecoming party because you are no longer away and separate. Yes, you'll have consequences for your decisions and need to be accountable to them, but you are no longer estranged from yourself.

Reconciliation puts you on the other side of the door where you are rejoining and reconnecting with you and all the parts of you. Now, it's time to turn your attention to the next level of acceptance—love. Love invites you to commit to and care for yourself and all your parts no matter what. It's where you take the pursuit of yourself seriously, not because you are perfect or because you earned it, but because it's what's best for you.

5

Love

*Love is the unrelenting commitment to the care
of yourself*

Love is the Acceptance of Self, Not the Denial of It

Did you learn like I did in your emotional education and training (also called childhood) to deny yourself, your impulses, your emotions, and whatever else made others around you uncomfortable? Oftentimes with good intentions, we were taught to take care of everyone around us before caring for ourselves, but then sometimes found out that our time to be taken care of never came.

As important and commendable as it is to be considerate of the needs of those around us, it is just as (if not more) important to be considerate of your own. This means that you need to accept that you do in fact have needs, and that those needs are as important as the needs of other people. Do you do as much to take care of your needs as you do for others? To deny you have needs or need any care is not healthy, it's neglect, and you must avoid this if you want to love yourself.

Remember, denial of the ability to have certain thoughts, impulses, behaviors, or emotions is to deny your responsibility for them. Without taking responsibility for them you'll feel like you are a victim of them. When this happens, your defense becomes, "I couldn't help it, I had no choice. My partner/ex/child/parents, or some supernatural being like the devil made me do it." It's a helpless way of living because it takes your power away because you gave your power away.

I remember as a child feeling tortured internally because I would think of a cuss word (especially terrible ones like "butt"), have a negative thought about God, or do something like flip off my brother. I felt terrible because I did not believe it was normal and okay to have those thoughts or experiences. In fact, I believed it was sinful and terrible, and maybe even eternally punishable (I'm not exaggerating!). So, by trying to avoid some future hell, I found myself in the present hell of self-condemnation. It's interesting because growing up I thought of hell as a place bad people go when they die, but now I see hell as a present experience of trying to meet an impossible set of demands or expectations. Had I been taught something different as a child, like it's normal to think of bad words, have all kinds of negative thoughts and doubts about God, and flip off your brother every once in a while, then I would have been saved from the torture of trying to save myself from myself. I've worked hard to make sure my children don't have the same experience.

Accepting that you will have all sorts of thoughts, inclinations, impulses, emotions, actions, addictions, and other challenges is precisely what allows you to face them. Loving yourself even though all of your thoughts are not pure and clean or all of your motives aren't perfect, that is love. Most of the time you don't even choose what comes into your head, and when you can be okay with that, you can accept it without denying yourself. Power in life does not come from being able to control everything within you, but from being able to respond compassionately to yourself regardless of what shows up in your brain.

Unhealthy Self-Denial Comes from Not Prioritizing Yourself

Before I go more in-depth about love, let's examine what gets in the way of it, starting with unhealthy self-denial. Healthy self-denial is when you deny yourself of something that can harm you or others or cause unnecessary suffering, from not eating that extra piece (or 3) of cake, to stopping yourself from criticizing or berating yourself or another, to leaving a situation where you might physically or emotionally abuse someone. Unhealthy self-denial is when you deprive yourself of something good (including healthy critique) or diminish your value by putting others ahead of you to the detriment of yourself.

How Do I Know if I Am Engaged in Unhealthy Self-Denial?

Below are some questions to help you identify if you may be struggling with unhealthy self-denial:

- Do you ever feel guilty for wanting to do something good for yourself?
- Is it hard to remember the last time you did something just for you?
- Have you had the experience of not being able to enjoy something because you felt guilty for taking the time and resources from your family to do it?
- Do you do everything you can to provide for the happiness and care of others, while rarely ever taking the time to treat yourself?
- Have you ever caught yourself thinking that you are enjoying something too much?
- Are you frequently the one in your relationships where you take on the brunt of the responsibility so that the other person can do what they want?
- Do you find yourself resentful of others because they get to do what they want and you don't?

- Do you often change your plans for others?
- Do you routinely say "Yes" to others when you really want to say "No"?
- If you have kids, do you find yourself so wrapped up in their lives that you have little time to live yours?

The more you answered "yes" to these questions, the more you may struggle with unhealthy self-denial and should consider how to increasingly make yourself a priority. Your work is to see your needs as being just as important as the needs of those around you, and then become more focused on your needs. At first it might feel like total selfishness (and others may tell you this as well because they benefit from your lack of self-care), but taking care of yourself is absolutely different from selfishness.

Expressions like "Mom guilt" represent self-denial. Mothers can suffer from feeling guilty or neglectful if they take any time for themselves. It especially doesn't help when a mom has a partner, parent, in-law, or friend who makes remarks about how neglectful she's being by taking time for her. Neither does it help to watch some other mother's social media feed who appears to be able to do everything perfectly for her children. Even in the absence of other's remarks, though, mothers can bring their own guilt, depending on what their belief of being a mother is. I hear mothers express guilt when they convey how it is almost not worth going out because of all the guilt they feel internally when they do. The single parent may also have a hard time with this idea of self-care due to all the demands of children, work, and life. Time is at an absolute premium, and to use it on one's self can feel wrong.

Self-care and maintenance needs to happen in your life, and to do so takes a strong commitment to making it happen. It is vital you make efforts to care for yourself, because if you don't, you will never do it. If you never care for yourself, though, you will eventually be forced in some way to take care of yourself through illness, mental breakdown, extreme exhaustion, threat of divorce, actual divorce, death, etc. Please don't be the person who has to be forced into self-care!

What if you could see treating and caring for yourself well as absolutely essential to your health? What if self-care is one of the most important acts of love you could do for yourself *and* others? What if you could feel confident in your ability and willingness to care for yourself?

Caring for ourselves shouldn't be something we have to ask permission for, but something that we see as one of our primary responsibilities.

Innerexia is Emotional Anorexia

If your life is full of unhealthy self-denial, you might be innerexic. *Anorexia* involves the withholding of food and nutrients from the self in an attempt to feel control through controlling weight. *Innerexia* is a term I made up to describe the withholding of nutrients of love and care from yourself in an attempt to feel control over your thoughts and emotions toward yourself. If you are being innerexic with the intent to harm yourself, it is a form of masochism (self-harm). If you are doing it in order to get the care and attention of others because if you suffer enough then others will take care of you, it is martyrdom. If you do it because it's all you know, it's probably just modeling (i.e., my grandmother didn't care for herself, and my mom didn't either, so this must be how I am supposed to do it). Sometimes it's a combination of two or even all three of these, which makes it even more difficult!

Innerexia is a rejection of love towards yourself coming from a place of insecurity. In many cases, I believe this insecurity is rooted in living in a culture and/or family obsessed with the outward appearance of success and happiness, with little regard for true inward happiness. With innerexia, instead of challenging your family or culture and its ridiculous pursuit of facades and appearances, you end up chastising yourself for not being able to succeed in your family or culture's games of vanity. Instead of rejecting the ideals of the culture or family and its misguided aims, you become a symptom-bearer of it.

Symptoms of innerexia include:

- Discounting compliments from others
- Looking at yourself in the mirror with disgust
- Injecting or ingesting things in your body to make you feel or appear happy when you are really not happy
- Believing you are ridiculous for having needs and wants
- Not speaking up for what you want or need and not taking responsibility for getting your needs met
- Ruminating on past failures and beating yourself up relentlessly for them
- Treating others with kindness and respect while treating yourself with harshness and self-hate
- Refusing to let yourself or others do nice things for you
- Tolerating abuse from others and yourself
- Experiencing a nagging sense of unworthiness
- Suicidal thoughts and attempts

Maybe you have some of these symptoms. I've experienced most of them in my life and fall back into bad innerexic habits at times. When you do indulge in innerexia, loving yourself feels nearly impossible, however, the way out is a matter of learning to love yourself just a little bit more each day. You do this by feeding yourself healthy psychological nutrients (love, care, compassion, grace, understanding, kindness, etc.) in your heart and mind. You might have to spoon feed it at first, but every little bit makes a difference.

Love is Not to Be Confused with Passion

When passion is confused for love, you not only get young adult vampire novels obsessed with undying lust, but also the advancement of the dangerous idea that if you don't feel a deep longing or desire for someone or something, you might not actually love or want it. The word "passion" has its roots in suffering, meaning to be passionate toward something means to be willing to suffer for it, almost as if not having it would be the end of you.

Love should also not be confused with passion because love generally operates more like a sedative to passion. Love calms passion down enough to keep passion from overrunning you so that you do something extreme or dangerous. When passion rules, you can end up harming yourself or others by making the possession of the object (even a person as an object!) of your passion more important than the respect and care of it. This can lead to "crimes of passion" like violence, manipulation, stalking, deception, or coercion. While passion is often what initially fuels the desire to pursue something, love keeps you committed to pursuing it (or not) with respect and integrity.

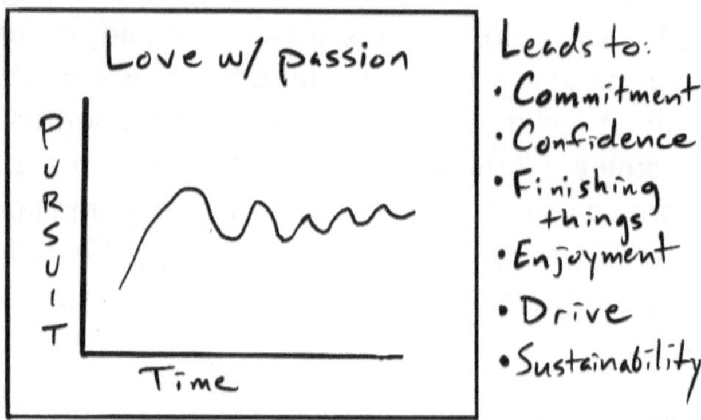

However, when passion and love come together in a healthy way, you experience excitement and energy. You're motivated by passion and committed through love. The passion waxes and wanes while love functions as the endurance and stamina to continue, and then passion adds a boost as a reward to your commitment. It reminds me of the space shuttle where a massive amount of fuel is used to get the shuttle out of the Earth's atmosphere. Once out of the atmosphere, the large gas tanks are released and the remaining fuel is used to course correct and boost as needed.

When the Feeling of Love and the Actions of Love Come Together, the Experience is Powerful

What if you have the feeling of love, but you're not showing loving actions? Is the feeling really love? Conversely, what if you're taking loving actions, but

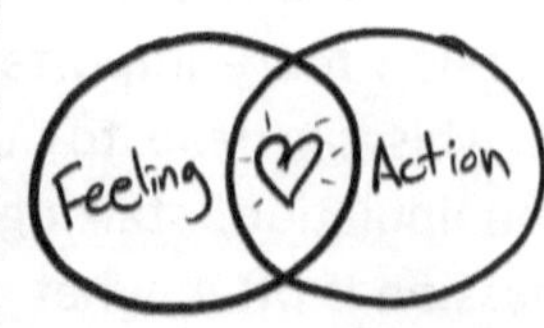

aren't "feeling the love"? Both of these situations imply you are having an internal conflict. You need to find a way to match your actions with your feelings, or vice versa, for a more complete experience of love.

Feeling plus action creates the most potent experience of love. You can feel love for yourself without doing loving things for yourself, and you can do loving things towards yourself without the feeling. However, when you get the feeling and action of love together, you notice a different kind of experience because your feelings and actions are finally aligned.

I'm reminded of Jack, a man in the second half of his life, who started feeling more love and acceptance for himself, but still had areas where his actions were not accompanied by the feelings of love. Wanting to change this at fifty years old he allowed, for what he told me was the first time ever, his wife and son to celebrate his birthday and give him gifts. While it was unnatural and awkward for him, it became a defining moment for him because his growing love for himself was matched with action.

While you don't have to do anything to prove you are worthy of love, the proof of your love will show through the way you treat yourself. If you say you love yourself, and yet denigrate yourself when you make mistakes, you've got work to do. Your love comes to maturity when the actions and feelings are in alignment.

Love is Unrelenting Commitment

Love is the unrelenting commitment to the care of yourself. And, if you've done and continue to do the work of reconciliation, there is more of you to care for and love. Once you're through the acceptance door it is love that keeps you there and makes it easier to remain in that place.

Love Depends on Understanding

The Buddhist teacher Thich Nhat Hanh wrote, "Understanding is love's other name. If you don't understand, you can't love." Leaving harsh, unkind judgment behind and encountering yourself with understanding and kindness is what it means to love. Criticism becomes curiosity, dread becomes discovery, and interrogation becomes interest in love. When "understanding is love's other name," you pursue yourself regardless of the conditions in your life. While there is a beginning to understanding and love, the end is only limited by your ability to stay interested.

This means you don't have to continue asking judgmental, dead-end questions like, "What's wrong with me?" and, "How could I be so stupid?", but rather you can ask understanding questions like:

- Why am I feeling this?
- Who am I afraid of letting down and why?
- Is this the truth, or is it my feeling at the moment?
- What can I learn from what I am experiencing?
- How can I better understand instead of rejecting it?

Also, when you fall back into an addiction or old patterns that you are not proud of, rather than hitting yourself with a barrage of disparaging and shameful questions, you should take a step back and seek understanding by asking compassionate questions like:

- What pain or emotion am I dealing with or avoiding?
- What triggered this feeling in me?
- What can I do or who can I call to get support?
- What can I do differently next time in order to avoid this situation?
- How can I take better care of myself?

Love is the Gardening of the Self

Gardening is an act of intentional planning and delayed gratification. You put in the labor up front knowing in time you will see the results of what you've planned and planted. The work is worth the results you will enjoy later, which makes the work as important as the results. You reap what you sow in gardening and in love.

Gardening can be overwhelming at first, just like love. You're faced with many choices upfront like when, where, what and how far apart to plant. Then, you have to figure out how to keep everything alive. However, if you stick to it for several seasons, you begin to develop a feel for it, and you become more proficient at it.

It's okay if loving yourself feels like work right now (because it is!) and it's overwhelming (but it won't always be!). Tying your shoes and writing an entire sentence was difficult and overwhelming at first, too, but now you can probably do them effortlessly. Do the work of loving yourself and you won't be disappointed, because taking actions according to what you want for yourself in the future builds patience, and this patience produces one of the greatest feelings possible—confidence in your ability to take care of yourself.

Let's look now at what the work of loving yourself is going to entail and how you are going to increase your confidence to keep doing it.

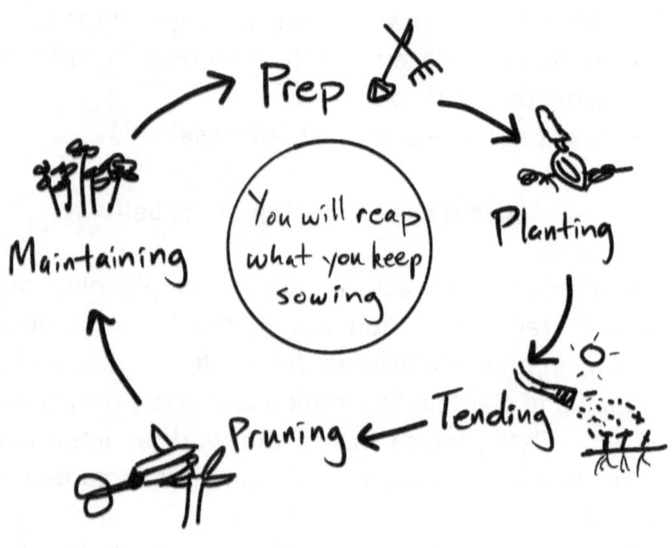

Preparation

First off, give yourself credit! If you have thoughtfully made your way this far through this book, you've done a lot of preparation already. Through tolerance, appreciation, and reconciliation you've prepared the space for you to grow in love. Furthermore, you are no longer merely hoping you will feel better, you are doing the work.

As the character Paul von Hartmann says about hope in the movie *Munich—The Edge of War*, "Hoping is waiting for someone else to do it." It's way easier to sit on the porch and imagine a great garden than it is to get your hands dirty and make one, just like it is easier to make a dream board and have aspirations for your life than it is to take the actions to make it happen.

Planting

We came to this work already planted in a time, place, culture, and family. The choice before us now is to determine if we need to dig up our roots and move or get down to our roots and grow where we are (currently) planted. Let's explore how we know which decision to make.

When Do We Dig Up Our Roots and Move?

When it's clearly dangerous. If you are being physically, verbally, and/or mentally abused you need to get help and find a way out. If any attempt to grow or change is met with abuse or threats of abuse or abandonment, including financial abandonment, seek help and make a plan for what to do. Someone else outside of you needs to know you are in danger.

You can call the U.S. National Domestic Violence Hotline at 1-800-799-SAFE (7233), online at www.thehotline.org, or text START to 88788, for support and help about what to do if you are in a dangerous situation.

When it's clearly time. If you are staying in a situation in order to avoid moving on to the next stage of your life, it's time to move. It's clearly time when the only thing growing is your dependency on others. If you are an adult dominating kids on the basketball court at the local junior high or making your mother prepare your lunch for work each day, it's time to move on in your life. I'm a fan of time-limited support groups because they give the group members a chance to heal and be supported, while also having a clear end date, at which members can evaluate where they are and if they need to continue in the group.

When Do We Get to the Roots and Stay Planted?

When it's clearly you. When you find yourself with the same problems wherever you go, it's probably you. It's time to accept you are the common denominator. For instance, if you can't seem to sustain any relationships and start to wonder why there are no good people out there anymore, it might be worth taking a closer look at *you*. Why might you be attracting these types of people? What can you do to be a better relationship partner? Get to the roots.

One time I complained to a friend over email about a problem in my life and I asked for his advice. He replied with his advice and I did nothing with it. In fact, a month later, not even thinking about my first email, I emailed him again about the exact same problem and asked his advice. What did he do? He sent me his exact response to the first email. When it occurred to me what happened, I realized the problem I needed to address most was myself, and I had to decide if I really wanted to get past my problem, or keep talking about it with anyone who would listen.

When avoiding it doesn't work. If your efforts to evade a problem have not worked or have only served to make the problem worse then it's time to go deeper and explore what needs to be addressed. I know I have the tendency to give up and move on when I run into difficulty. Unfortunately, my escape doesn't get rid of my problem, it just moves it down the road for me to run into it later. Only in facing it and figuring it out can you ever make progress.

Unless it is unsafe—clearly dangerous—you can move forward into the work of tending to yourself.

Tending

We all know most plants thrive with water, good soil, and sunlight, but let's be honest here, how many plants under your care have you watched meet their untimely demise? Maybe you've even avoided having plants at all because you aren't sure you can keep them alive and healthy.

Tending creates tendencies, because how you tend to care for yourself (or don't) will determine your capacity to do it consistently. Nothing can substitute for actually doing good things for yourself and taking good care of you. Our brains love repetition and predictability, and we have to make choices about what to reinforce. Now is the time to create loving tendencies in your life and reinforce them with repetition and positive feelings.

Similarly, most people go through life without any type of intentional care and then get frustrated when they are not happy, healthy, or thriving. This would be like not watering a plant and then being mad at it for not producing healthy green leaves.

Look at your own life. If you are not taking loving actions toward yourself and are frustrated because you don't love yourself, is it because you are not doing what you know you need to or are you avoiding it because you aren't sure if it will make a difference?

Either way, if you are not doing it, start...and start small. Don't freak yourself out by trying to do too much at once, your brain does not do well with a lot all at once. Choose one thing, like meditating five minutes per day or going out once a week to do something you enjoy, and do it consistently. You don't need a love fest, you need small, sustainable, loving habits. Love yourself in small ways and build from there.

If you are avoiding loving and caring for yourself because you aren't certain it will matter, it's okay to "try it before you buy it," but you have to do the "try it" part. I encouraged a client of mine, Heather, to spend 5-10 minutes every night checking in with herself and the different emotions she noticed during the day, not to judge herself or her emotion, but to be present and accepting. She incorporated this simple action into her life, and it increased her acceptance and love as she felt more in control and at peace with herself. Don't underestimate the power of starting small.

Tending to yourself is also about environmental improvement and management. Since you adapt to your environment, the internal and external space you live in is of high importance, because you will either expand in the space you are in or shrink to fit in it.

Have you heard the story about how a goldfish's size is determined by the size of the tank around it? It turns out this is only partially true. The truth is the goldfish's size will be either stunted or realized based on the size and environment of the tank. Goldfish in small tanks or fish bowls are smaller because their growth is stunted, causing them to be unhealthier, smaller, and have shorter lifespans compared to their counterparts who live in more spacious and suitable environments.

We are not goldfish, but we can and do suffer a similar fate. We don't always realize the fishbowl that we've put ourselves in or that has been put around us by others, but we can see evidence of it in our lives, in things like fatigue, chronic illnesses, hormonal imbalances, low energy motivation, difficulty experiencing pleasure, anxiety, daydreaming about living other people's lives, and feeling helpless and hopeless about changing our own lives. If we don't turn things around and increase space in our environment for more love and acceptance, we'll never realize our full potential or be able to find the freedom and energy to effectively and consistently pursue our growth.

When you've created the conditions for growth through tending, it's time then to decide how to reinforce your growth, and you do that through pruning.

Pruning

You can let a plant grow wild and let it become what it will. However, in some instances this comes at the cost of the plant not growing as strong or healthy as it could. When you learn how to prune a plant, you are learning how to trim away parts of it so that other parts will get more resources and energy to grow. Pruning is choosing where to direct the limited energy and resources needed for growth.

Fortunately, you are not a plant, and the pruning you have to do is not actually cutting off parts of yourself. What you must do is choose what is best for you and be willing to part with what is not (even if it may not be that bad).

Love begs us to ask the honest questions, "What am I going to value the most and put my energy into for the my greatest good?," and, "What am I willing to allow or receive in my life to help me grow?"

If you can't or won't decide to do what is best for you, you will hamper your growth. Because of your indecision you are going to enable growth-inhibiting factors like addictions, bad relationships, high risk activities, angry outbursts, bad financial decisions, and conflict avoidance into your life. While you have other good qualities and behaviors, they will be hindered because the energy will go to managing the outcomes of your poor decisions, not to the growth of your positive qualities and choices.

Sometimes the choice is between a good thing and a better thing. You might want to keep your beloved motorcycle, but might need to consider if it is best given your circumstances, or you might have to choose between a job with more travel or less travel, and depending on your circumstances, neither is necessarily a wrong choice, but one might be more beneficial for your growth depending on your values.

The choices you make between good/better are a reflection of what you value. What will increase your growth most is the integrity you create as you align your choices with your values. Only then can you put your energy in the direction of what seems best for you, even if it means letting go of other things.

Perhaps you find yourself in what is called the "I don't know" trance. The trance is induced by starting sentences with "I don't know why," or asking over and over, "Why do I _________?" Once under the trance it's as if you can't figure anything out. Whether it's why you procrastinate, have affairs, lie, rage, eat too much, always show up late to things, the "I don't know" trance results in feeling helpless unless you can figure out why. The trance could be indication that you need to go deeper with some guidance from someone outside of yourself. However, if your search for the why keeps coming up empty, then it's probably time to prune it.

For instance, if you are waiting to start healthier habits like eating better and exercising because you don't know why you can't seem to make the healthy changes, and your therapist or TikTok videos aren't helping you make sense of it, it might serve you better to go ahead and stop (prune off) the pursuit of why. Then, you will have more energy to put into developing your new habits. Pruning is a decision to stop pursuing a "why" that so entrances you, so you can pursue what you need to do in order to move forward.

While getting to the root of things is important, it's not ultimately what will make you change, just like seeing that the roots of a plant are unhealthy won't change the plant. Doing something differently is what will help create change regardless of your knowledge, or as Milton Erickson, a famous psychiatrist once wrote, "Change will lead to insight far more often than insight will lead to change."

Maintaining

When you get your garden in good shape, the work shifts then to maintaining it. You do what is necessary—continue to water, keep pests away, and other things all while you simultaneously enjoy it and care for it. As basic as it sounds, you have to keep at it if you want to keep it.

Maintaining your life involves continuing to watch what comes in and goes out of your life and making adjustments as needed, taking stock of your relationships, and paying attention to your thoughts and emotions. It means making sure you are taking time to care for yourself. This would include things like eating and sleeping well, connecting with your community, expressing gratitude, and nurturing your relationships, among other things. Oftentimes it is just actually doing the things that you already know you need to do.

The more you practice maintenance, the more it becomes automatic, like any habit. People who love themselves don't do it by accident, but by practice. I strive to be this way and hope you will too, because it gets easier the more you do it.

It's a Moving Cycle

Where are you in this self-gardening process? Each part of the cycle is as important as the others, and moving through them is what brings growth and maturity. Stay in one too long and you can get stagnant, while skipping a part or blowing through a part can give you less than optimal results.

Are you always prepping and never planting? Maybe you've done all the therapy, read all the books, been to the conferences, then gone to more therapy, and watched TED Talks, but still haven't taken any serious steps. If this is the case, it's time to plant—to actually make a commitment and take action in your life.

What if you planted (by taking some action) but aren't seeing the results you want? Or you've taken some action and stopped? This means you've got some tending to do by bringing into your life what is good for you and then being patient as it takes root. If loving yourself is a new endeavor it might take a little longer because you are starting from scratch.

Have you grown to the point where you've got to decide where to focus your energy? It's time to prune! For instance, by loving yourself more you may realize that you need to make changes at home, work, and with friends. You need to decide where to focus your energy so as not to get overwhelmed by all the growth. It's like a business outgrowing the staff's ability to support it. It's great to grow, but growth comes with the responsibility and necessity of deciding where you are going to focus your efforts.

I have a tendency when I am pruning an actual tree or bush to go *way* too far. It's so cathartic I can get carried away, only to have an "Uh-oh" moment when

I've realized I've almost trimmed everything off, usually accompanied by my wife exclaiming, "What'd you do to my tree?" A little word of warning: Don't prune in mass like I do to my shrubbery. Instead, make strategic and premeditated decisions on what you are going to trim out of your life so you can focus on what you are deciding to make central to your growth.

Finally, you can find yourself perpetually in the maintenance phase. Your life is going well, and all your effort goes to maintaining and protecting it. However, without any new challenges you might get stagnant and bored. When people stop focusing on growth in their lives, they tend to pursue pleasure and/or comfort, which can stifle growth. For example, you may find yourself in a job you don't really like and that brings you little joy or fulfillment, but you stay in it because it is comfortable enough or allows you to pay your bills and maybe even buy whatever you want. As a result, you do what it takes to make it through the day and keep the paycheck coming in, but it doesn't do much for your soul. The mid-life crisis is the quintessential example of someone stuck in maintenance too long and needing to grow.

When stuck in the maintenance phase it is easy to forget that the seeds for next year's harvest come from the current harvest. Enjoying the harvest and planning and investing in the next season is what keeps the cycle productive.

Grace Clears the Way to Love

Grace is love's superhighway. It clears the way to love like no other concept, which is why it is present in most major religions and taught by most spiritual teachers (or at least the ones who are worth listening to).

Grace is letting go of the responsibility for your human condition so you can be free to take responsibility for how you live with your human condition. Grace allows for you to love yourself while you struggle with something. The addict must learn to love herself before waiting to no longer have the addiction or impulse.

Another type of grace is what I call beforegiveness, which means forgiving yourself *in advance* of failing to be perfect. It's saying to yourself when you wake up in the morning, "I'm going to fail in some way today. I won't meet an expectation of mine or someone else, and I am going to forgive myself in advance." This doesn't mean you deny any responsibility for your actions and have no guilt for anything. Grace means you accept your fallibility and humanness, so when you mess up (which you will until you die), you meet yourself with love rather than shame, which makes it more likely you will take responsibility for your actions, especially if they hurt you or others.

If you struggle with loving yourself, chances are you need more grace. You need to surrender to the fact that perfection or flawlessness are not prerequisites for love, they are impediments to it. You can't make yourself worthy of love, only receptive to it.

Love is the unrelenting commitment to the care of yourself, and grace clears the path.

Re-Parenting is How You Grow Your Love

Love is a kind of re-parenting of yourself. It's providing your adult self a kind of parent who supplies your life with the nutrients you need to feel loved and grow. When you, like a child, have the nutrients of positive attention, healthy boundaries, kind treatment, and calm adult presence (especially when all of the things are coming from you!), you will thrive.

You might find it more difficult to give these loving things to yourself as an adult if you did not get them much as a child. To complicate it further, you've probably reinforced your negative beliefs about yourself and your downplaying or denial of your need for good love and care through the choices you've made and your relationship patterns. You're likely replaying the old narrative of not being good enough or not being worthy of love because it's what you know.

If this re-parenting idea is a stretch, can you imagine yourself loving and caring for a child? If you can, this means you at least have an idea for what to do. If you can't, find somebody who can teach you. The next step is to start from whatever ability you have and then practice it. Give yourself the love, care, and understanding you would offer a child. Chances are you needed the same love as a child and this is your opportunity to either experience it for the first time or re-experience it if it's been a while.

In this way, love is like building muscle—you work your muscles in order to get stronger. It doesn't matter the strength or size of the muscle before you start working out, only that you start working out with what you have.

Love calls you to do for yourself what you would do for anyone else you see as worthy of love. Since seeing yourself as acceptable and worthy of love has been your journey in this book, what's left is growing your ability to do it through practice.

Forrest Gump

I've watched Forrest Gump once a year in the fall for several years now to remind me what it means to live with integrity and presence, and also to fantasize what it would be like to live with the absence of a critical voice in my head. The main character, Forrest, who many see as "stupid" ends up living a monumental life, not because of IQ (his is low), but because of how he lived his life present and free of self-judgment, condemnation, and shame.

Lieutenant Dan, on the other hand, represents the antithesis of Forrest. He is a born leader and a tough-as-nails kind of guy. He knows his purpose and how to achieve it—serve his country and die in a war like the men in his family before him. For him this unfortunately does not come to fruition because instead of dying, he is saved by Forrest, but not without the loss of his legs. He comes completely torn apart internally. He spends most of the movie violently fighting with shame and hatred. His character sits in stark contrast to Forrest, who is not at conflict with himself and instead takes life as it comes with little resistance or attempts to control it.

Two majorly different ways through life illustrated on screen. In one scene we see Forrest and Dan on a boat in a hurricane. Dan is cursing and calling God out, while Forrest stays at the helm of the ship. In other scenes we see Dan drinking, contemplating suicide, and hiring prostitutes while his life breaks down, and Forrest taking life as it comes, pursuing the woman he loves, as he allows her to come in and out of his life.

One of the final scenes of the movie is Forrest's wedding. Lieutenant Dan walks (he's since gotten prosthetic legs) up to Forrest, and in his usual uninhibited way, Forrest remarks, "Lieutenant Dan, you got new legs." Lieutenant Dan stands there smiling, makes a joke about his legs, and introduces his fiancé. All of this to represent Dan finally coming to a place of peace with himself and his past.

As much as we would like to function like Forrest with an uncritical mind and unfettered optimism, and some days we might even pull it off, we are oftentimes more like Dan. The question is which Dan are we going to be–the Angry Dan or the Loved Dan. We can criticize ourselves, judge ourselves, be victims of our past, and beat ourselves up on our way through life because it didn't go as planned. Or, we can learn to love ourselves, accept ourselves and our pasts, and find peace in who we are, regardless of what life has brought us.

Finding the One

Has anyone ever told you that you were the "one"? What a pedestal to be on! Were you able to stay on it? Did you ever stop being the "one" for that person?

Or... have you ever told this to anyone else? Being so sure that you finally found the person meant for you forever, you crowned them with this awesome responsibility: *The One*. Out of 7+ billion options you found the one. What are the chances? I had a friend who found the "one" three times before he got married to the "one."

Still, I believe in finding the one, and it won't surprise you at this point in the book when I tell you that the "one" to find is none other than *you*. Your partner is not the "one," the person you broke up or who broke up with you last week was not the "one." You are the "one" for you, and depending on where you are with yourself right now, this could be exciting or terrifying, liberating or paralyzing, energizing or exhausting, or some mixture of all of these.

I have good news for you if you are not in a loving place with yourself: nothing else about you has to change except the way you see yourself. Loving yourself is not about changing you into something better, it's about changing the way you see yourself. Think of what changes when you see another person as the "one." The person might as well be glowing! Imagine seeing yourself like the "one", because you really are the one who will always be with you. As the "one" you stop seeing yourself as someone to change, and start seeing yourself as one to cherish, value, pursue, and enjoy.

Finding yourself is not a one-and-done event, unless you plan on never changing again. Love is about committing to yourself and going on the adventure to find yourself over and over, accepting of the changes. The more you find yourself, the more you find to explore. It's like getting to the top of a mountain peak, looking out, and seeing other peaks waiting for you to climb and explore.

6

Liked

Liked is the experience of being both present with and delighted in yourself

We're at the Top!

Liked is the top of the acceptance pyramid and the final destination made possible by all the work you've done up to this point. I believe many people stop at love because it's what they've been told is the top. You could absolutely stop at love and experience a great, fulfilling

How it all began (circa 2007)

life, or you could continue on to the even more fulfilling experience of being liked.

When it comes to navigating the best possible relationship to yourself, like is what you crave the most because this state is acceptance fully realized and experienced. By escaping the trap of basing your acceptance on perfection, performance, pleasing others, or anything else external, you are free to like yourself. You can still feel a desire for the acceptance of others, of course, but you no longer need it or depend on it.

Social media creators figured out how important acceptance was to you and have exploited it ever since by the addition of one little feature: the "Like" button. Often represented by a simple thumbs up icon, the "Like" button remains one of the single greatest inventions ever created to engage humans in any activity. Getting a "Like" in the social media world is the ultimate acceptance, and it is the most valuable social currency of our day.

The "Like" button is so powerful you must take it back for yourself and learn how to click it in your own life. When you are liked by you, you no longer need to get likes from others.

What is Liked?

Liked is the experience of being both present with and delighted in yourself. While loving yourself is about caring and giving, liking yourself is about delighting in yourself. It's the ability to be at home and comfortable in your own skin, as if you are returning to a time before you learned to be overly self-conscious or ashamed of yourself. You might even be experiencing it for the first time.

Fortunately, liking yourself doesn't require the absence of any negativity in your life. Even when you have a critical voice in your head (which we all have, it's just that some of us are able to take it less personally), you can still like yourself. Do you still get depressed and anxious? No problem, because you don't have to resist or eliminate feelings anymore in order to accept yourself. You might even find yourself enjoying your ability to see what's going on in your mind because you are no longer driven by it or feel a need to eliminate it.

The Dynamic Duo of Love and Like

"I love you and I like you." Isn't this what we all long to hear? The combination of love and like is powerful. To be loved *and* liked by someone...is there a better

experience? When you put love and like together towards yourself, you feel and experience several things. First, you feel an increased internal comfort as you feel little or no need to be any different than you are in the moment. Second, you are more present in what you're doing because you're not judging yourself. Finally, because of those two, you get to enjoy yourself.

One of the difficulties long-term relationships often face is not maintaining love, but maintaining like of each other. You change, the other person changes, life conditions change, and while the commitment is there, the enjoyment can fade. However, finding a way to enjoy the person again can reinvigorate the relationship. In the relationship with yourself, this can happen as well—you stop liking yourself over time, but then find a way to enjoy yourself again, which leads to a greater satisfaction of life.

"I love you, but I don't like you." Isn't this what we all dread to hear? It's one of those statements that's confusing when someone says it to you, but makes total sense when you say it to someone else. What you are essentially saying is, "I care about you, but I don't enjoy how I feel around you." It might also be a way of saying,

"I'm committed to loving you, and it is that commitment I am upholding, but outside of that, I'm not feeling much enjoyment of the relationship." I love a lot of people who I don't necessarily enjoy being around, and if I had to choose someone to hang out with when I was bored, I wouldn't choose them first.

"I like you, but I'm not in love with you." This is also possible and usually reserved for people who bring some joy into your life but you don't have much of a relationship outside of being entertained by them. I like the comedian Jim Gaffigan, but I don't feel a need to care for him. He brings me joy, but I don't make him soup when he's sick, because that would be a bit creepy.

My point is how awesome and extraordinary it is when the dynamic duo of love and like are working together in your life. The experience is divine in the one-with-myself way, as a sort of coming out party of the accepted self. Shame has moved out and acceptance has moved in. If we're looking for the nirvana of acceptance, this is it.

"I Love and Like Myself"

How does it sound when you say aloud, "I love and like myself"? (No seriously, give it a try right now.)

I often feel some inner resistance to be quite honest, and I know it comes from growing up with a fear of what would happen if I enjoyed myself too much. I feared I would become conceited, greedy, and prideful, so I've spent a lot of energy throughout my life trying to avoid coming across in all those ways.

After the resistance subsides, though, I smile, realizing that my fear has not come true. Choosing to like myself has not made me an egotistical narcissist. In fact, when I make it more important to be liked by someone else than for me to like myself, I act in ways that are much more selfish and narcissistic. I pretend to be someone I'm not in order to get the other person to like me, and even if it "works," it's not really me they like, just the pretend me.

When you put love and like together within yourself you become free to be yourself with yourself and with others. You get to have an internally liberating experience, like the one you have in a relationship when you finally stop pretending and start showing up as yourself.

Liked is When You are Like a Child and Grandparent at the Same Time

Have you ever been on the receiving end of grandparents doting about their grandchildren? It can be annoying and endearing depending on how much time you have to listen. They see the best in their grandchildren and they want everyone to know about it.

My grandfather had a bumper sticker *inside* his late-1980's station wagon on the glove box. It read, "If I knew grandchildren were this much fun, I would have had them first." I loved sitting in front of that bumper sticker as I rode with him, because it was about me, and it told me that he enjoyed me.

I hope you had grandparents who had enough separation from the responsibility of you to simply delight in you. With people who had the generational space to be with you and not in charge of you, one of a grandparent's primary roles is an enjoyer. In fact, what often makes this relationship closer is you have a common "enemy"—your parent (and their child!)–who you can defeat through enjoyment.

In the same way, what happens when you like yourself is that you are able to experience life like a child who is uncritically and joyfully alive, while simultaneously looking on with the enjoyment of a grandparent. The overly-responsible, serious parent stays away. When you spend more time in like, you will feel less need to do the serious work of changing or fixing yourself, and more desire to engage in the playful work of being you.

By the way, what would your internal bumper sticker say– the one that reminds you of who you are? Mine would say, "For fun's sake, enjoy yourself."

You Have a Million Chances to Make a Good Self-Impression

When you act out of who you are, you feel pride. I get great joy when one of my daughters comes up to me with one of her creations and proudly waves it in the air proclaiming, "Look what I did!" I could care less about the "quality" or usefulness of the project because that is not what matters. What matters most is what it means to them, and they impressed themselves by what they did. Liked is about impressing yourself more than anyone else, or as I'll refer to it, making a good self-impression.

Making a good self-impression means that you impressed yourself because you are being true to yourself. You are acting out of who you are and what you want without anyone else's permission. Few things feel better than impressing yourself.

Fortunately, you have limitless opportunities in your life to make good self-impressions, so if you miss one, you'll instantly have another one. If you let yourself down in one moment, you can impress yourself by being true to yourself in the next moment. Whether it is an action you take (or don't take), a thought you have, an idea you come up with, or something you produce, you have an opportunity to be impressed by it. In a world where something only seems valuable if you can monetize it, an act of impressing yourself can feel like an act of defiance—you did something for you and you alone. Are you willing to do things even if someone is not going to buy it or like it on social media? Even if you are able to monetize your creation (which is not a problem if you can), the experience of joy in your creation can't be touched (or made!) by money or outside approval. So, the question is this: how will you impress yourself today?

Self-Like is the Most Reliable Kind of Like

I need to confess something to you, and maybe you can relate to this: When I like something on social media or in a text and give a thumbs up, it doesn't always mean I actually like it. The places my mind goes and the strange algorithms I run through before giving a "like" is a bit complex (code for "neurotic"). A like can mean a lot of things. Here is just a partial list of why I've clicked the "like" button in the past:

- I wanted you to like me because I liked you.
- I wanted you to see I liked it so you'd think of me.
- You liked something of mine and I felt a need to reciprocate.
- I thought what you said was clever and I wanted you to know I was clever enough to get it.
- I truly liked what you said or posted.
- What you posted made me laugh.
- I was trying to click something else.
- I wanted other people to see my like.
- Everyone else was liking it and I wanted to fit in.
- I actually loved it, but I was afraid a heart button might give you the wrong idea.
- I wanted you to feel good about yourself.
- I wanted you to keep commenting on my posts in the future.
- I liked someone else's comment above yours and didn't want to feel like you thought I didn't like you as much.
- It was easier to like something than to actually tell you what I thought.

A really messed up form of like often comes down to either ego protection or social positioning. Again, I'm not proud of myself here, but I am doing it to make a point: you can't completely trust my "like" of you because you don't actually know my, or anyone else's, true intent behind it. It doesn't mean it's untrue, it's just not always reliable (or clear!). I am also not saying you can't feel good about people's likes, just that you can't let their likes (or lack thereof) determine your like of yourself.

The most reliable like is your own because you know your intent, and it is hard to fake yourself out. Narcissistic people are the exception because they fake themselves and others out by creating an image or persona to like instead of being who they are. Whether aware or unaware of their deep insecurity, narcissistic people try to force themselves and everyone else to accept the (carefully curated) image that they are putting out. However, since the image turns out to be a mirage, it doesn't work. Instead of accepting that the image is a mirage though, a narcissistic person will often do whatever it takes to convince everyone that the image is real. When being liked is more important than being truthful, a person will remain subject to image management and the relentless protection of it at all costs.

If you are capable of liking yourself without demanding it from others or convincing them to like you, you are not in the narcissist category (congratulations!), and you get to live your life as an expression of you.

Expect Resistance When You Express Yourself

A fair warning: when you enjoy and accept yourself, you will often experience resistance from others and even from yourself. Because most people don't live like this, it's normal for you and others to feel uncomfortable when you do. Self-expression can be met with social rejection. Your work is to keep it up!

Paradoxically, what communities resist most is what they often need the most: people who know who they are, what they want, and aren't afraid to pursue it. People like this make sure communities don't get too stuck in their ways. You would think this would deserve a celebration, but it usually doesn't happen that way. One of the hardest parts of being yourself is resisting the urge to shrink yourself whenever someone takes exception to your new found freedom in being yourself.

My charge for you is to keep being you, fully expressed. Remember, liked is not about being a better version of you, it's about being more fully who you already are. You will make others uncomfortable when you are living out of your true self, but by doing so you are also giving them permission and even inviting them to do the same. Your life is challenging their assumptions about what it means to be alive, and if you show them a different path, they might get curious and want to begin to experience it for themselves

What your relationships need is a fully-expressed you who is unashamed, and not a compliant you that hides in fear. You must seriously and playfully learn to both accept and like yourself. If you don't express who you are and what you want, you might rely on someone else to do it for you, and then everyone would miss out on what you have to give when you choose to simply be yourself.

Performance Minus Outside Demands Can Benefit You

Studies have shown that when people look at an artist's commissioned work and non-commissioned work without knowing the difference, they tend to like the non-commissioned work better. Something about removing the demands or expectations of a patron seems to have an effect on the artist's work.

Julie (a past client) and I were talking through what brings her to life since she reported feeling lifeless. After some thought, a smile came to her face, and she brought up dancing. "I didn't like performances. What I enjoyed most was when our teacher would dim the lights, turn the music on, and tell us to dance however we wanted." No expectations, no one watching, just dancing and moving in whatever way she wanted without an audience. With the demands of a performance removed, she was free to come to life.

Liking yourself is non-commissioned art and a dance with no one watching. Nobody is paying you, watching you, or demanding anything from you. Your responsibility is doing more of what lights up your soul. Whether it is for an audience or not, it is always for you first.

Non-Commissioned Living is About Expressing Yourself

What's one way to take the joy out of something? Make it into a job, have customers with demands, and then do whatever you can to get positive Google reviews. I bet you've heard stories about people who enjoyed something like cooking, photography, painting, making furniture, or working on cars until it became a commissioned (paid) activity. Once the activity became something they "had to do" for someone or something else, it made it impossible to experience the same kind of enjoyment they had when doing it because they wanted to do it. All of a sudden, they had new, different, and uncontrollable expectations from themselves and others about how they should do their work.

This is not always true, of course. I know people who have found the sweet spot of enjoying themselves, liking what they do and who they work with, *and* getting paid to do it. They've found the holy grail of loving what they do and a market willing to pay for it.

Regardless of a paying customer or market, the fullest expression of ourselves in our work is where satisfaction and enjoyment reside at the deepest levels. My goal in life and work is the same: to be me as much as I dare to be. I don't believe we need to grow beyond ourselves, we need to expand to fill ourselves. Shrinking is what we need to avoid.

I want you to make life about expressing you. It's the most important creative act you can do. You might not be able to do this in your day job or chosen career (although you might be surprised if you try it), but there are certainly other ways. Can you remember something you enjoyed doing as a child, but gave up at some point because it wasn't seen as important or commercially viable? Maybe you quit doing something because you heard someone say something like, "You can't make money as an artist." Examples of things to get your mind started are drawing, writing, thinking up jokes, acting, dancing, singing or playing an instrument, poetry, taking a walk, gardening, solving math problems, or making up silly games. What if you took up something that used to help you express yourself again? Several years ago I started drawing and making up birthday cards for all my family members because it was a way for me to express myself. Now, I express myself more with drawings, including doodling in this book.

I invite you to engage in more non-commissioned activities and see what happens. Since you are already opening up more space in your life through acceptance, you might as well take full creative advantage of it. When somebody, or a voice in your head, tells you something you are doing is not marketable, say, "That's okay, I'm doing it for something far more valuable than money... I'm doing it for me."

The Space to Like Yourself is Created Through Differentiation

Differentiation is the ability to make a distinction between two or more things. If you aren't able to differentiate between you, your thoughts, and emotions, you are incredibly predictable, whether you think you are or not. If you consider the emotions you are experiencing as negative, you'll likely react with resistance or avoidance in your unique ways. If you label the emotions you are experiencing as positive, you are more likely to accept them and want them to remain. If you wanted to, you could even write a book about how you react to your emotions and title it, *When I Feel This, I Do This*. When you give a special signed copy of the book to those closest to you they would say, "Thanks, we already know." One of the hardest parts about writing the book would be realizing how much you are like your parents in ways you promised yourself you wouldn't be, but that everyone else notices.

What allows you to like yourself is the space you create through differentiation between you, your thoughts, and emotions, whether they are negative or positive. With this space you can learn to delight in the perspective you get by not being driven by what is going on in your mind. When you make this shift in your brain you have a removed playfulness, like when you see your favorite band or musical group perform, to enjoy yourself.

Like Can Be a Practice or Performance When Judgment is Not Central

My wife and I like to play ping pong for different reasons. I play for the fun of it and could care less if we keep score. She wants to play and keep score because she enjoys the competition. She doesn't see a point in playing without keeping score, while the enjoyment of playing is the point for me. So who's enjoying it more?

Funny enough, when it comes to running, my wife cares very little about running races and trying to set personal records. What she loves about running is getting to do it with another person. It's a social event for her and she enjoys the shared experience. She hates running alone. I, however, grew up watching my brother win race after race and constantly go after faster times. I wonder why someone would run without wanting to push themselves to hit or beat certain times or opponents. The same question applies: Who's enjoying it more?

In both situations, neither person necessarily enjoys the activity more, because what matters most is how the activity is being experienced. Like can be found in practice (doing for doing's sake) and performance (doing it for results or an audience). The key factor comes down to judgment. By judgment I mean the critical evaluation of worth based on an outcome. You can enjoy ping pong or running for competition because of the competition, but if you have a lot of your worth and validation tied to the outcome, you'll only enjoy it if you win or hit certain times. Likewise, the practice of playing ping pong or running for fun stays enjoyable when it's about the experience of it and not the validation of your identity or skill. The more you rely on something to determine or confirm your value, the more power it has to *devalue* you.

Our society values the experience of winning so highly that it's easy to think it's what will make us like ourselves. It doesn't, at least not in the long term anyway. If it did, Michael Phelps, the most successful swimmer ever, would be the happiest man alive, not dealing with crippling depression. Michael Jordan, one of my childhood heroes, should be the most satisfied person ever, but in any interview I've seen, he still seems disappointed he wasn't even better than everyone else. A friend of mine who has been very successful would be proud of what he's done, not depressed because he hasn't been able to achieve the same level of outward success again. We should be able to have a poster that states, "When you achieve X, you can feel successful," and feel satisfied when we reach it. However, the sad truth is the X in our culture is filled in by the word, "more." You can never be enough when the expectation is always more.

Like is the practice and performance of being yourself without judgment, the need of validation, or the need to be more. When you realize you are enough, you won't have to be any more.

Like is a Responsible Action, Not an Irresponsible One

Liking yourself is not a license to leave everything and everyone else behind in pursuit of yourself in an irresponsible manner. It's the permission to pursue yourself and the enjoyment of yourself while also maintaining your responsibilities for yourself and to others. You might find yourself making some dramatic shifts in your relationships and environments, but liking yourself is a thumbs up to you, not a middle finger to those who are vulnerable or depend on you. Although, at times it might very much feel like, and even be, a metaphorical middle finger to the expectations and demands that you have felt from others.

I encourage you, unless you are in a dangerous or abusive situation, to like yourself where you are for some time, and give you and others around you an opportunity to adjust. Don't leave your kids if you are a mother or father, rather find a way to let them see you liking yourself. By liking yourself and staying connected to them you are giving them the best gift you can, and one that they can learn to give themselves as they grow.

Liked is Acceptance Fully Realized

I played the trombone from sixth grade until college. The reason I picked the trombone was purely based on infatuation. The sixth grade band teacher came to my elementary school, picked up a trombone, blew a loud note through it, and then made the pitch go up and down by moving the slide. I was mesmerized, and I *had* to learn how to make that noise.

You see, to me the trombone was initially a means to doing one thing: making the same beautifully raucous noise I just heard. In the beginning I had no idea it would become one of the most enjoyable parts of my life and provide me with a group of friends and a place to belong during some very dark years of my life. My first day playing in a jazz band in ninth grade nearly knocked me off my feet in amazement. The powerful outcome of a decision I made in fifth grade became fully realized years later in ways I could not have known when I made the decision.

Twelve other kids chose to play the trombone in fifth grade, but only three of us played through high school. We were the ones who realized the power and possibility of our decision in ways the other nine didn't. Similarly, liking ourselves sounds like a great goal to aspire to, but then there's the work it takes to get there and realize it.

Liked is acceptance fully realized for those who make the full journey through tolerance, acceptance, reconciliation, and love. It's reserved for those who push through the internal resistance coming to all who decide to challenge long-held beliefs and patterns of living. It comes to those who stop believing everything they think and feel and instead seek out truth. Liked is a dramatic act with dramatic consequences only experienced by those who are willing to enact the full story of acceptance rather than hoping for something magic to happen like in a fairy tale.

How do you know you are not merely becoming infatuated with yourself or the idea of liked? Simple. You don't quit when it's difficult and wait for someone or something else to get you there.

Liked has More to Do with Experience Than Performance

This level is more about experiencing yourself than it is performing, because even in performing, it's about how you experience the performance. Liked values experience over performance, and presence over perfection. In a deep place inside us, I believe we know when we are experiencing like. We feel a resonance within ourselves. However, here are some markers suggesting that we are experiencing this level.

Amusement with yourself. This means being loose and able to laugh at and with yourself despite what you've done or how well you did (or failed to do) something. Mistakes become missteps that can make you chuckle. You're humored by life and your attempts to live it comfortably, and you may be especially tickled whenever you have a thought that you have anything totally "figured out." Instead of covering up your insecurities by becoming a character who appears to

enjoy life, you actually enjoy life with all the insecurities, which paradoxically makes you more secure.

Bob Goff calls this experience "whimsy," which, "... needs to be fully experienced to be fully known. Whimsy doesn't care if you are the driver or the passenger; all that matters is that you are on your way." Whimsy embraces the experience of life and your part in it, which is why Bob also cleverly points out, "Life is like a sweepstakes, you have to be present to win."

Experiences of flow. Mihaly Csiksgentmihalyi wrote in his book *Flow*, "It is when we act freely, for the sake of the action itself rather than for ulterior motives, that we learn to become more than what we were." I would argue we don't become more than what we were, but we become more of who we are, and we become more engaged in the act of being ourselves.

Flow means engaging in an activity or experience with no other goal or reward than the experience itself. It's when you are least self-conscious and most present in something. Effort and time seem to move effortlessly as you engage in something meaningful to you. The activity can be anything you do. I routinely find myself in flow when I'm writing or drawing cartoons and I look up to see an hour went by and it felt like minutes.

Calmness of mind. Our minds don't typically stop. The term "monkey mind" from Eastern philosophy is a great way to think of what our minds do automatically: they grab at anything shiny and available in the moment. The more emotion you are feeling, the more your monkey mind grabs at whatever it can. You can't defeat or control your monkey mind, but you can become an observer of it. When you like yourself, you are able to engage the monkey mind playfully instead of only trying to defeat it. The monkey mind is there for your amusement.

Calmness of mind, then, is not the absence of a monkey mind, but the presence to observe it. You don't stop your mind, instead you see what it's doing, and don't worry too much about what it grabs. You differentiate yourself from your mind so that you can exist peacefully with it.

For me, it's like being on vacation and being present even as my monkey mind is reminding me that I have to leave soon, and I have work next week, and I won't be back here for a while, and I've got to make more money to make up for what I spent on this trip, and I have to figure out my entire life in the next five minutes... and on and on it goes. With calmness of mind, I am able to find my way back to the present (it can take me a while, too), and then find amusement in the funny things my mind does.

Diminished need for extrinsic rewards and motivators. When you are able to do things simply because they are important to you, even if they are not as important to others, you are liked. Sure, you might be so proud or amused with what you created or thought up and want to share it, which is great, but you don't need the other person to like it in order to justify liking yourself. This is important in my case because the ideas, jokes, or cartoons I come up with are often met with confusion when I first share them. I have grown quite accustomed to the blank look on my wife's face when I explain to her my latest idea or creation. If I need someone to understand or like them, then I'll filter my thinking too much. Is a joke funny only if the audience laughs or an idea valuable only if others get it, or is it enough that you came up with it and like it? I once heard the psychologist Jeffrey Zeig say, "In heaven they tell jokes, and in hell they explain them."

Liked is when you find yourself doing what you choose to do because the reward is found in taking the action, not the goal of the action. It's learning something you are interested in, not because it is going to be on a test. In our age of social media, it is doing, eating, drinking, drawing, or watching something even if you are not going to post about it. What you do matters even if no one else knows about it.

An inner smile. It is easy for most people to smile on the outside even if they feel terrible on the inside. We've mastered the fake smile and we get fooled by it all the time. I am always a little surprised when people are shocked that some public figure who appeared to be happy confesses that they struggle with serious depression or worse, dies by suicide. It seems to me that we should be just as worried about people who appear to be really happy as those who don't try to hide their despair.

When you truly like yourself you don't have to fake the appearance of liked on the outside anymore, because you have an inner smile. You can't see the smile, but you feel it on the inside as a peaceful sensation. When you are liked by you then you no longer have to worry about what gets displayed on your face, because it will take care of itself.

Liked is Letting Go of the Character

We've all created and constructed, consciously and (most likely) unconsciously, a character for others to like, and we've been reading the character's lines ever since. The character is searching for external significance and love, and will do whatever it takes to get it, but often settles for something less—flattery, codependence, Facebook "Likes," superficial connections, or a promise of love.

Years ago, psychiatrist Carl Jung wrote, "Don't hold on to someone who's leaving, otherwise you won't meet the one who's coming." In more pop culture terms, the saying goes, "If you love someone, you have to let them go."

Both of these statements express a profound truth: if you are holding on to something too tightly, you aren't open (and can't be open!) to anything else. You can't like yourself if you are holding on tightly to a character who is not you. You and your audience may like the character, but unless you let the character go, you won't be able to meet the one who's coming, the accepted you.

You need to be like the Hollywood actor who is only offered one type of role because he or she is so good at it, but desperately wants to play something else. The actor must resist taking the old role in any form, even though the easy paycheck and the red carpet await. As the offers either get bigger or probably more frighteningly, stop coming at all, only in continuing to refuse them will there be a chance of a new role. In your case you have to resist accepting any role that is not you.

I won't set you up for impossibilities. Can you be totally character-less? Probably not, but you can be less of a character and more of you. You need to wear less masks. To go to bed knowing you were more of yourself and less of a character means you are liking yourself

Liked is Your Home

Those who like themselves are one of earth's greatest treasures. When I look for friends, mentors, coaches, therapists, or spiritual teachers this is my primary focus. I want to find people who are at home with themselves, because being in their presence inspires me to do the same.

Ram Dass said, "We're all just walking each other home." This statement touches something deep within me. I believe our home, the one we left when we stopped accepting ourselves, is a place of love and like for ourselves. Home is the acceptance, the enjoyment, and the like of ourselves, and one of the reasons we exist is to show each other how to get back home.

Liked is your home. It's where you came from, it's where you are returning to, and it's where you can live.

7

The Journey Forward

Take a Look at Where the Journey has Taken You

It's not what you can do for acceptance, but what your own acceptance can do for you. Take a moment to look at your own journey over the course of this book. We've traveled from the pits of self-hatred and contempt through the vast expanse of growing your acceptance, and up to the mountain to the final destination of *Liked*.

Every journey changes you. You can't return to where you came from as the same person you once were. Up to this point, I've intentionally made the journey entirely about you and I've encouraged you to keep the focus on you. I did this because I believe what your family, friends, and the world need most *from you* is for *you to accept you*. Your acceptance gives you the freedom to bring yourself more fully to all of your relationships, rather than some character who is trying to be accepted.

When you live *from* acceptance, you no longer have to live *for* acceptance. All the important areas of your life like your relationships, your career, your religion, your mental health, are transformed when you come from a place of acceptance rather than a place of neediness for acceptance. You can come to all of those things more fully alive and expressed.

Once you are the primary source of acceptance for yourself, you get to take the higher levels of awareness and responsibility you have for yourself and share them with others. You won't even have to tell others about the work you did, they will experience it through how you live.

Let's take a closer look at awareness and responsibility, as they are now two of the most important tools for your continued acceptance, and how you continue to live into this experience of being liked. Then we'll talk in depth about what this means for your relationships. Finally, we'll end with instructions for you moving forward.

"Stayin' Aware" Makes Continued Acceptance Possible

Throughout life you are going to continually make mistakes and slip back into old patterns. No one is immune to this. No one. Not even the big-time motivational speakers you see jumping and dancing around on stages avoid this. Why do you think they keep jumping around and teaching others to do it? It's a reminder to themselves to stay the course. *Liked* is a destination you get to, but it also takes intentional effort to stay there. You will go through ups and downs and lefts and rights, but it is staying focused on the practice that matters.

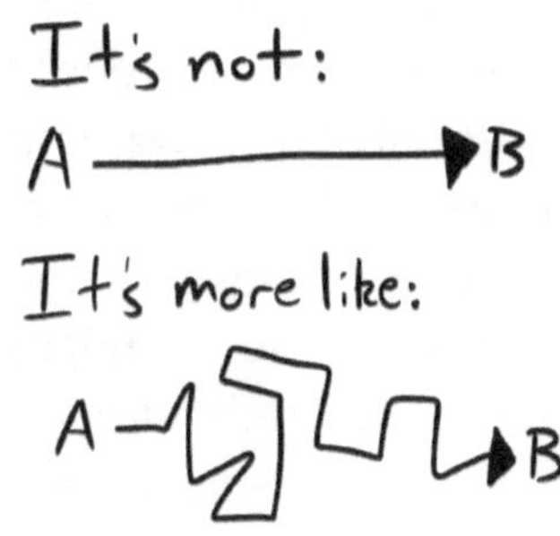

A boat going from New York City to London doesn't go in a straight line. The route is affected by factors like weather, wind, waves, tide, and other boats. The captain steers the ship through a series of course corrections based on the conditions it encounters, and then it arrives at its destination. Staying on the course of acceptance is similar, and as the captain of your ship, you must continually make the corrections to arrive at Liked. And this is where awareness comes in...

While the Bee Gees sang, "Stayin Alive", the song I am singing here is, "Stayin' Aware." When you commit to "Ah, ha, ha, ha, stayin' aware," you are able to make course corrections as needed because you can see the conditions around you and respond to them. For instance, you might find yourself over-invested in trying to gain someone else's acceptance, and with awareness, you can catch it and change what you are doing. You might catch yourself slipping back into trying to please others at the expense of yourself and your values, and awareness helps you take a pause and create space to address it.

"Stayin' aware" means you continue to stay curious about yourself and your behaviors. In doing so you create an opportunity for something other than a predictable emotional reaction to take place. When you tolerate and pay attention to the thoughts and feelings you have, your awareness of those thoughts helps you decide what you want to do next. The negative, shame-filled thoughts and feelings you might experience don't have to be resisted when you have greater awareness, instead, you can simply respond with thoughts like, "That's interesting. How can I use that to help me understand more about what's going on?"

Awareness is what helped me through writing this book. I realized why I've said for twenty years that I wanted to write a book, but never did—it put me in a position to be judged or evaluated (code words for rejected). Early on in my writing I found myself writing two books. The first book was the one I wanted to write because I had a message to share. The second book was the one I felt like I had to write in order to please everyone. I had to give up on the second book or risk becoming schizophrenic, because if I tried to become all things to all people, I'd have to be 16 different people at once.

At the end of the day, though, awareness created the distance I needed to see what was going on while I struggled with it. Okay, awareness *and* my writing coach, Michael, because sometimes awareness means knowing when to ask for help. Michael and I had some good laughs at my self-induced craziness and stereotypical writer's melodrama. He asked curious questions in the face of my suffering, which helped me stay playful and engaged. And ironically, he would remind me to follow my own advice.

Awareness allows you to continue the work of acceptance so you can take responsibility for it.

Responsibility Makes Continued Work Powerful

Remember that responsibility is a combination of two words, "response," and "ability." It means you have the ability to respond to something (versus only reacting to it). This entire journey has been about increasing your ability to respond to thoughts, feelings, fears, and anxieties in ways that lead to acceptance rather than judgment.

Through awareness comes greater responsibility for what you've realized about yourself. When both of my children accidentally and innocently used cuss words for the first time, like rhyming with words like bit and truck, we laughed and thought it was cute. No intention, no problem. Afterwards, my wife and I explained to them why the word they used was not a word we would like them to continue using, especially in social settings. When they intentionally used the word after knowing what it meant, we held them more responsible for its use (and sometimes still giggled about it). It's the same with us. Awareness provides opportunities for responsibility, and even a few laughs.

This is why one of the most impactful and transformative actions you can take now is continuing to grow your responsibility through your awareness.

In the Bible an unwillingness to accept responsibility was wrapped up in the first recorded sin. After Adam and Eve ate fruit at the urging of a snake from the one tree God told them not to, and then they attempted to avoid all responsibility for their action. Eve blamed the serpent, Adam blamed Eve, and I would have blamed reverse psychology (telling them not to eat it made it almost irresistible). Regardless of the excuse, God countered their unwillingness to take responsibility with substantial consequences, including the permanent revocation of their membership to the Garden of Eden.

I feel a deep connection to this story because it mirrors one of the greatest "sins" in my life—to make someone or something else responsible for me. When I give away the responsibility for myself or my decisions, I cut myself off from the power I have in my life to choose how I am going to live.

Nothing has had a more robust effect in my life than taking more personal responsibility. I remind myself of this often because it is easy for me to fall back into being the victim of life, rather than the force behind my life. Responsibility is what keeps you and I in the driver's seat of our lives.

What You Have Done for Yourself, You Can Now Do for Others

Can you imagine how your relationships would be if you accepted yourself first and then accepted others the same way? What if curiosity and compassion became the main way you interacted with all people, including yourself?

Maybe, like me, you might still feel selfish and guilty when you focus on yourself first. For me this came from a life of being praised for my "humble servitude." Don't get me wrong, I am glad I helped others. Serving others gave me a way to get outside myself and feel good about myself for what I was doing. Ironically, the care I was showing others was the care I was wanting to experience, I just needed to serve myself as well.

When you realize that care and service for yourself is as important as the care and service you provide or want to provide for others, you become more generous and beneficial in your relationships, because you are giving out of what you have rather than what you lack. It keeps you from trying to get from others what you need to give yourself.

This is why, "Love your neighbor as you love yourself," is a powerful truth. You've got to love yourself well if you are going to love your neighbor well. If you don't, you'll love your neighbor as a substitute for loving yourself.

So get out there and love yourself well, knowing that you can apply these levels to others because you've applied them to yourself. Tolerating, appreciating, accepting, loving, and liking are all yours to extend to others, rather than things you are trying to get from them. You can now give out of your abundance instead of giving out of your need (which is really taking if you think about it).

Remember, before the journey, you asked others to do the work of acceptance for you. You wanted others to like you so you could like yourself. And by the way, this is often precisely what it took to set you up for liking yourself—being liked by someone else. When you experienced the love and acceptance of somebody else, they gave you an invitation to be the same way toward yourself. The question then became whether you would accept the invitation to love and accept yourself or would you continue to hold them responsible for making you feel it. Continuing to hold them responsible *for* you would be like detaining and taking hostage your mail carrier the next time he or she delivers your mail (a felony offense, so don't do it!), rather than simply receiving the mail.

When you accept and love others, you are delivering a message to them about their worth and value. As long as you don't get stuck taking responsibility for how they feel about themselves, then they can work on taking their responsibility for it. The power of love and acceptance for yourself, and then to others, is the power to inspire others to love and accept themselves.

As a human, you're created for community. You will still want others to accept you and approve of you. I mean, please keep practicing good hygiene, being kind to others, and showing up to meetings prepared, even though you are still acceptable (but maybe not enjoyable) if you don't do those things. The point is to no longer need or demand acceptance from others. Your value does not need to derive from outside factors like performance or perfection, but from the internal belief, confidence, and security in your own inherent value. Internally-derived value and acceptance is yours to keep, and the desire to love others that comes from that value is yours to give.

Six Final Pieces of Wisdom for Your Continued Journey

I gave you instructions in the beginning, and now I want to give you a few more words of wisdom for your continued journey.

Don't only look up, but also look down so you can see how far you've come. Whether you simply read this book cover to cover, or only looked at the pictures, or took your time and worked your way through it, stop and take note of your progress. When you started, it might have been hard to see the top, but from where you are now, what do you see? How's the view? What's now behind you and what's ahead of you? As you looked up the pyramid, the question was, "How am I going to do each level?" As you look down, the question is, "How can I keep doing what I learned on each level?" What makes me most excited for you is knowing that if you apply what you read, you'll benefit from it. I want liking yourself to feel natural, and the only way to do that is to keep doing it until it becomes automatic.

If you are stuck or struggling at any point, it's never too late to increase support. Have you come across anything that you feel like you need help working through? I hired a professional coach and writing coach while writing this book because I had never written a book, and I knew the support would be invaluable. I had to work through difficult emotions and thoughts to write this. I would have still written something, but it would have been the same aimless writing like I had done for years, and I would have filed it with all my other journals. Before these coaches, my journey involved therapists, friends, pastors, mentors, and others, the best of which refused my attempts to make them responsible for me, but rather guided me on my path. Good helpers don't take you out of your suffering, they come alongside you in it and walk with you through it.

In rock climbing, the command "on belay" is used by climbing partners or guides to indicate that they have you supported by ropes, and it is safe to climb. Their support is something you can trust as you climb up, knowing that even if you slip or fall, their counterbalance will keep the slack tight so you don't fall too far. In addition, this person has a perspective you don't because they are below you and can see what you can't. If you are stuck, perhaps it is time to find someone you can trust to be "on belay" for you. They can't (and won't) climb for you, but they can (and will) support you while you climb.

Embrace turbulence because it means you are in a position to grow. I'm not saying intentionally create drama in your life and kick the proverbial hornet's nest. We call that reality TV. I mean embrace difficulties and challenges because they are what will help you grow the most. You will be challenged by your thoughts and emotions that come up about accepting yourself because you are attempting to have new thoughts and emotions. The old ways of thinking and feeling won't give up easily, because they were what you believed kept you protected in the past. This book is offering you a way to look at your life that should make you uncomfortable if you haven't yet accepted yourself. However, discomfort is what challenges you to encounter your views and see if those views are still what you want to follow. Discomfort, if you will engage with it and not avoid it, is an opportunity to make changes in your beliefs and thoughts that aren't serving you well anymore. If the turbulence is too much and you need help, reach out.

You create momentum by taking action, and momentum is addictive. By the way, if we were motivated primarily by knowledge, we would all be eating, sleeping, and exercising better. Doing something with the knowledge we've obtained, taking action on it, and then seeing the benefits of our actions is what motivates us and creates momentum. In this way, momentum becomes addictive and we continue to take action.

Action got you here and action will continue to move you forward. A willingness to do what it takes to accept yourself and then feeling the love and like that comes from that acceptance has the ability to create a lot of positive momentum for you. Stop doing good things for yourself and you'll lose the momentum, or worse, create momentum in the other direction.

Keep telling yourself your new stories, and update them as you go along. Your old negative stories are hopefully coming to a close and are being replaced by new stories of acceptance. You might have been a victim of the old stories, but you are the hero of the new stories, and as such, you will continue to face challenges and learn lessons on life. If you remain the hero of your stories, you will reinforce the narrative that you are in control of your story, not because you control everything that happens to you, but because you decide what things mean and how to use them in your story. Write a

story about how you use life, not how it uses you. Make adjustments as necessary. Write. Live. Edit. Repeat.

A Final Word

You are no more acceptable right now than when you started this book, but I hope you are more accepted and *liked*...by you. Your acceptance of yourself matters the most. Once you've solved your acceptance problem, self-hate won't make sense anymore. When you live at *Liked*, you're free to fully realize yourself and bring yourself to the world, and we need you!

Thank you for caring enough about yourself and others to take this journey. Let's find our way to *liked* and start living there!

What do you see?